# Unity in the Faith
## What Keeps It from Happening?

Bradford Mark Rosenquist, Ph.D.

WESTBOW
PRESS®
A DIVISION OF THOMAS NELSON
& ZONDERVAN

WestBow Press books may be ordered through booksellers or by contacting:

WestBow Press
A Division of Thomas Nelson & Zondervan
1663 Liberty Drive
Bloomington, IN 47403
www.westbowpress.com
1 (866) 928-1240

Scripture quotations marked RSV are taken from the Revised
Standard Version of the Bible, copyright © 1946, 1952, 1971 by
the Division of Christian Education of the National Council of
the Churches of Christ in the USA. Used by permission.

ISBN: 978-1-9736-3420-1 (sc)
ISBN: 978-1-9736-3419-5 (hc)
ISBN: 978-1-9736-3421-8 (e)

Library of Congress Control Number: 2018908244

Print information available on the last page.

WestBow Press rev. date: 7/27/2018

# ABSTRACT

# Unity in the Faith: What Keeps It from Happening?

The whole idea of there being one church ... one Body of Christ is undeniable when one reads the words of Jesus, and the letters of Paul the Apostle. Yet today we see a Church Universal scattered across the globe with an incredible variety of names for their group of believers, often intentionally separating them from other groups of Christian believers. There are efforts across the nations to bring the churches today together with conferences, seminaries and conventions, if not, intentionally separating to establish "non-denominational" groups with the apparent intent to get away from the implications of the denominational environment of being cloistered into a group with a special set of additional traditions and secondary beliefs and protocols that make them feel that they are on target with the Bible and Jesus.

We have at least 1600 incorporated groups (denominations, associations and other organizations) across the United States alone, much more when all nations are included. Each of these groups has a history. Each of these groups has developed over time, often based on the work of a single individual, such as the first pope (Roman Catholic), Martin Luther (the current groups with the title Lutheran in the church name), and Billy Graham (the Billy Graham Association), and other evangelical groups and pentecostal groups. Certainly the groups of Christian believers are affected by geographical locations, such as the Anglican church (Great Britain, England), and large associations (such as the National Association of Evangelicals in the United States for the most part). Each group continues practices that establish the continuance of their group ... traditions, understandings of biblical beliefs, and protocols that have historically proven to be a means of retaining and keeping the congregation together. In western nations, like the USA, it is also a matter of living in a constantly changing culture that impacts and influences each successive generation. So, the leaders of the Christian groups are constantly reassessing the ways in which the church conducts its services and teaches the biblical principles for Christian growth on a personal level as well as on the organizational level. Issues of finances, paying mortgages for the facilities in which they meet and responding to the dictates of the huge number of governmental departments (from the Internal Revenue Service and the state tax demands, as well as, being able to conduct the business of the church in reference to contracts with builders, electrical maintenance and such business as advertizing in local radio and TV companies.

Too often the time devoted to promoting unity within the congregation is more attentive to self-promoting Issues, and not the overall call of Jesus to do that which unifies the church universal. Getting to that end, requires a complete overhaul of what it taught in the local services and bible studies. The leadership must look to Jesus and the writers of the New Testament for guidance toward allowing the Holy Spirit of God to empower the individual born-again believer in his or her quest to be in union with God and all other Christian believers, regardless of culture, race, language and international or even community locations. God sees all believers in Jesus as one, so the church groups have got to focus on seeing their role as promoters of unity in the Body of Christ, as taught each week in the local congregation. Every believer is critically important to their part in the Body of Christ … all are essential to the work of the Gospel.

# CONTENTS

# PREFACE

One would think that being together on the same page, so to speak, is a critical strategy for any group or organization. In the automobile manufacturing business, whether in the United States, Germany or Japan, there are commonalities that are unavoidable. There are obvious issues of competitiveness, but that is openly expected and dealt with by making our automobile a little better than the next one: less expensive, finer appearing, better gas mileage, etc. But there is an established set of unifying factors that bring them together in the long haul. The fact that they all use petroleum products to function and that they need to ride on tires creates a state of unity that is rather foundational to the entire global producers of human transportation.

For some the description just presented, on a practical level, based on common practices in the essential automotive industry, may be too indirect in defining "unity." So, it may be necessary to go to a more direct example in our United States economy today that involves most everyone in some entertaining environments. The whole industry of professional baseball or football uses unifying practices throughout. Deviation from these protocols will end up creating such issues as suspension and even expulsion. As much as the competition is extreme in so many descriptive ways in the course of the actual actions, activities and execution of the game, the protocol for how it is played is what makes it the sport that it is. It is recognized as baseball and football by all who have the slightest familiarity with each of these sports.

The conflicts in Christian denominations, one with the other, as to the need to remain separate and not do what they do in a cooperative effort to reach the world with the truth about Jesus and the Kingdom of God, are not like the sport situation described above. No, these denominational differences if compared to, say the sport, baseball, would be a case of using a football to pitch to the batter, and the catcher would kick the baseball back to the pitcher. Such differences in sport would be so obvious that the spectators would stop watching and the players would no longer participate. Yet, in the overall picture of Christian churches, one can easily see wholly different ways in which the teachings are presented, to the point that one named belief does not register as comparable in the next Christian group. With over 1600 separate Christian groups, denominations, associations and fellowships, it is hard to grasp just how much of a contrasting difference exists from one end of the groups to the other.

The question then arises, "Why are there so many differences ... why must they be organized separately ... why must they establish a boundary between themselves and all other Christian groups. Taking it all to the height of confusion, one will be absolutely flabbergasted to find that one group will declare that another group really isn't Christian. It is believed that unless a certain set of beliefs are not adhered to, then the particular Group either missing a particular belief or has a belief distorted [that is how it would be Described if not just like their version], then they cannot be truly Christian.

It is sincerely hoped that by the conclusion of this book, it will be established as to what the real problems are that undermine unity across all Christian groups, and what must be instituted to begin to bring Christian groups together as a united front presenting the Gospel (Good News of Jesus Christ, the Savior of Mankind) to the people of this world who do not know it.

# INTRODUCTION

Recently, the Billy Graham Evangelistic Association presented a nation-wide program to promote a major effort to reach people with the message of salvation. Dr. Graham was determined to take final efforts to inspire the people who are Christian believers within all the congregations and associations/denominations that advocate Christian belief to make a greater effort to get the message of the Gospel of Jesus Christ more of an effort than is currently believed to be executed. The appeal was to those within the Christian ministry to reach out to their congregations and associations and even military groups to promote a much greater evangelistic effort, both on an individual level and as congregations and associations/denominations, representing Christ's standard message. One could certainly recognize the legitimacy of the BGEA effort as a genuine reflection of both Dr. Graham and his son Franklin Graham. The reports from US news media were quite minimal. Just what the results were from the reports back to the participants within the congregations and denominations across the United States and elsewhere has yet to be presented. Based on the typical distractions, disagreements and separate protocols that are extant from one denomination to the next, it is likely that the participation and efforts of cooperation were not what one would expect from people who all claim to be of the same origin in belief and action ... the Word of God ... the Bible. The

Bible is, in almost all cases representing the beliefs of a particular church congregation and/or local congregation, the defining declaration of what constitutes being the truth about Christian belief. Of course, the exceptions are those that are labeled as "cult" or "extreme," such as the Church of Jesus Christ of Latter Day Saints, and Jehovah Witnesses. Other such groups would include Christian Scientists and "Snake Handlers" who often locate in areas of eastern Tennessee, Kentucky or West Virginia.

According to the Pew Forum on Religion in Public Life, there are now in the United States alone over 1,200 denominations/Christian groups. The latest surge seems to be in the category of "non-denominational" or "cross-denominational." For the purposes of Internal Revenue Service recognition (taxation exemptions, etc.) each of these fairly new corporations of Christian believers designate their statement of beliefs and establish their relative status to other mainline denominations, such as United Methodists and Southern Baptists. As each new cross-denominational group is formed, another separation from basic idea of a unified Christian church is established. The question is simply this: "Does this undermine Christian unity as declared by Christ in John 17, or is there another way to describe the continuing separation of Christians into more self-determined Groups?"

## The Book Proposal

It will be the intent of this book to determine whether there is an actual need for Unity in the Christian Church (universal), as described by Jesus in his prayer to His Father God in John 17. If, in fact, it is determined that such unity is required by Jesus and the admonitions of the other writers of the New Testament/Covenant texts, then what is it that must be done to facilitate and execute that commandment/directive from Jesus? It will be the intent of this book to describe the current status of unity within both the Body of Christ (the Church universal), and what is the status of unity within any particular congregation of Christians, either as independent groups or a part of a larger association.

## The Background for this Proposal

Along with the determination of what constitutes "unity" within the Church Universal, it will be the intent of this book to describe representative examples of efforts to unify the Church of God, the Body of Christ, over the past twenty centuries, as demonstrated in history. A careful review of the New Testament texts will set the stage for the initial issues of unity or disunity that began at the outset of the newly established Christian church, or the "Way" as described in Acts of the Apostles.

On the other end of an historical review, will be an effort to declare the more current indications of unity and disunity in our modern times, due to the much more sophisticated and complicated technologies and inter-relationship of nations and cultures and other influences, such as media and entertainment as a part of a larger world culture. That culture of today … the twenty-first century … 2,000 years after the return of Christ Jesus to His Father in heaven … is not the same scale of impact as was in place during the time of the church being initiated on the Day of Pentecost in Jerusalem. In many respects it is logarithmically more intense and pressured than then.

## The Purpose of this Study

It is the purpose of this study to declare the current status of "unity" in the church across the entirety of the Christian faith. After all, Paul's admonition in Ephesians 4: 4-6 and verse 13, asks for "unity of the Spirit" first, then "unity of the faith." So, it is going to be critical to define the meaning of "unity" in those contexts of faith and Spirit. If there is a clear commandment from Paul as a direct extension of the words of Jesus in John 17, then it is essential in this study to spell out how that unity was to be executed and maintained throughout the centuries across all the geographical locations in which the church universal, the Body of Christ, was to develop as the admonition of Christ to go into all the world and preach the gospel would be carried out.

## The Significance of this Study as to its Benefit to the Body of Christian Knowledge

Over the years, for any believer of the Christian faith, there have been questions as to why there are so many segmentations and selective groupings of Christian believers. One certainly understands, without too much effort, the impact of geographical and cultural/language differences on the context in which any believer must live their lives. It takes a very small amount of investigation to see that, for example, that the Southern Baptist Convention is not so-called due to geographical issues alone, and that the impact of USA Civil War was a matter of significant influence on such a name for ???

# CHAPTER ONE

# Unity Defined within Christianity

Defining any word in the English language can be a complex process. For many words like the word "unity" which at the first seem rather common and fairly easily understood in most contexts, it can be deceiving as to the realization that it has a number of variant modifications in the Webster's Dictionary. It is a word which most people would not necessarily need to look up to find out what it means, in contrast to a word like "propitiation." Yet both are words associated with the Bible as translated to English from the Hebrew and Greek. The dictionary defines "unity" as: "the quality or state of not being multiple: oneness." It is not ended with that definition. There are six other major meanings for unity in the dictionary (Merriam Webster Collegiate, p. 1369). It goes on to state: "a condition of harmony: accord; the quality or state of being made one: unification; a totality of related parts: an entity that is a complex or systematic whole; any of three principles of dramatic structure derived by French classicists from Aristotle's Poetics ... ; a 20th century American religious movement ... emphasizing health ..." As one can see, being able to define a word in its proper context is essential to gaining the best understanding of its meaning for that particular comment.

As we move on to define "unity" as used in key texts of the

New Testament, it is best to go to recognized publications/texts in which this work has been accomplished by those who are experts in language translation from Greek to English. The Greek text is given along with the NRSV text and a literal rendering of the English parallel to the UBS, third edition. The referred text in the Gospel of John, is in chapter 17 where Jesus prays that the disciples would not only be kept safe from the world and Satan's influence, but be "ONE" as "We are one." The origin of the desire for unity is based on the fact that Jesus reminds not only the disciples, but the leaders of the Judaic religious bureaucracy that He only does the work that the Father has given him to do, and speaks only the words that the Father has given Him to speak (Jn. 12: 49-50 and 17: 21) (McReynolds, p. 402-403). Specifically, Jesus states in John 17: 20-23, "I do not ask on behalf of these alone, but for those also who believe in me through their word; that they many all be one; even as You, Father, are in Me and I in You, that they may also be in Us, so that the world may believe that You sent Me. The glory which You have given Me I have given to them, that they may be one, just as We are one; I in them and You in Me, that they may be perfected in *unity,* so that the world may know that You sent Me, and loved them, even as You have loved Me."

It is from this marvelous portion of Jesus' prayer to this Father God, that we derive the most powerful declaration of the significance of the impact of the need for unity in the Church, or Body of Christ. Christ is declaring that the ultimate relationship that He has with the Father, is the same relationship we are to have with Jesus and the Father, and with one another. Since we all as sons and daughters of God are, therefore, brothers and sisters in the Body of Christ, we need to establish unity in every way that we can by the power of the Holy Spirit within us as born-again believers.

When we are confronted with the statements of Ephesians 4: 1-24, where Paul tells us that through love by being patient and humble we are to promote unity through the power of the

Spirit of God. He reminds us and the Ephesian brethren that by grasping the fact that there is only one of the following: body of Christ, baptism, Spirit, calling, Lord, faith, God and Father, that the oneness of all that God is and has proclaimed necessitates unity. Even the established roles in the church are for the ultimate promotion of the "unity of the faith." The Apostle Paul urges us to see that our constant daily effort is to become more like Christ in everything so that the body of Christ "grows for the building up of itself in love." When the Apostle John declares in his final three letters that "God is love," it is simply a reaffirmation of the unified proclamation of Jesus to His Father as He knew He was about to leave this world, and needed his disciples to continue in every aspect of maturing in the Spirit of truth.

When one thinks of the basic meaning of unity, it is likely to generate other terms related to it, such as, words like: union, cooperative effort, collaboration, family unit, team effort, submission to the directive, maturing in oneness of mind, etc.

If we think for a moment about the effort of coaches in sports, we are reminded of one of their most fervent admonitions to each member of the team, unity of effort for the goal of winning. For the vast majority of who live within the borders of the United States of America, there has been some sort of competitive experience in which the individual was a part of a team effort to complete a task, win a game, or cooperative get something completed over a period of time. During the activity, there was usually one or more who was responsible to seeing to its completion, and not just to get it done, but to do it in a way that created at least some level of excellence, improvement or compliance with expectations that were for the most part generally known.

One of many books written about the Yankee all-time great, Mickey Mantle, entitled, "The Last Boy: Mickey Mantle" (Leavy, p. 202) addresses this pervasive need for the members of the group, team or enterprise to work together, putting aside individual desires, goals and personal need for acclaim in order to gain the success of the goal they are in a group to accomplish. Twenty-seven world series championships did not happen by chance. Those on the Yankee team recognized the key to success: unity. The protocols of sports, or business or any other entity that involves the collaborative efforts of people to be a part of accomplishing any agreed upon activity requires a number of characteristics that reflect a striving toward a unified action. There is the need to understand what the ultimate goal is to be or look like. Likewise, it is not always easy to describe the goal or interim objective or steps toward that goal. Take the example from "The Essential Drucker" (Drucker, p. 215) in which he uses the typical designated medical jobs in a hospital, a variety of specialists, each trained specifically to their unique essential role, yet they must collaboratively work to any one patient with total exactness to the whole medical need. No administration of service to that one patient can be done without a holistic grasp of its intimate impact on the entire bodily system of that patient. Obviously, the unity of effort is a constant pursuit so as to create a total resolution to the entire medical need the patient has. From surgeon to nurse to x-ray technician to the pharmacist the entire service plan must be in complete accurate and intentional protocol. Any decision for any variation must be addressed to the entire staff in one set fashion or the other. As is addressed in the text, "Communicating at Work," the key is collaborative planning at all levels and stages of a business, corporation and any other form of team effort (Alessandra, p. 98-99). Those who lead, provide guidance in any oversight or supervisory role, must be the ones to state and restate the goal and intent and details to arrive at that goal.

They must make that goal clear, understandable to the point that it can be restated by those being supervised. It must be real and that make that goal real and understandable to those who will work cooperatively to that end. We call them the leaders.

Leaders can go by many names, including, coach, manager, supervisor, guide, supervisor, guide, chairman, president, dictator, prime minister, and within the church, any variation of elder, pastor, priest, monk, father and related or modification of the same. So the entire context and environment of what we are addressing in the pursuit of unity, involves many elements within the practice of human endeavor. In the context of the United States public schools, the pursuit of unity is a constant debate and effort to implement and correct. At the beginning of the nation, the need for teaching the basics of reading and math became apparent, and local communities provided the most concrete training after need for education gained credence in the minds of most all groups of the people in the colonies and eventually the separate states. It was all based on the United States Constitutional statement that whatever was not specifically for the federal government was then the right of the state to pursue and implement. For the past 237 years education has slowly and persistently developed to the point that for most children and adults educational opportunity exists for most as a reasonably inexpensive opportunity. During the life of Abraham Lincoln the effort to organize and establish criteria and the specifics of instructional content also evolved through many cooperative efforts. The goal was often revised to include new areas of career and job preparation so that the individual could legitimately accomplish the pervasive goal of being a responsible member of the community, and a well-prepared citizen.

As the continuing need for unity in the nation was realized, even enduring a deadly civil war, the nation strove to continue in unity. Mr. Lincoln's intent after the massive impact of the Civil War was to bring unity in many ways. He had experienced as a candidate for the Republican party a remarkable effort of party organizers to promote him as the unifying candidate for the newly established political party (Bacheller, p.404). Eventually there were 50 states, each one a part on an equal level with the rest.

The United States of America represents a reasonable example of the effort to establish and maintain unity in the context of the world today.

Ironically, the United Nations is a seemingly parallel example to the USA, but many would take great issue with that, as the only apparent representation of unity is the willingness to send a representative to the city of New York, New York to present the issues their nation is pursuing. The actual review of the intent and accomplishment of this body of nations is their attention to matters that would facilitate their own nations benefit. There does not seem to be any real effort to join together under one union. The 195 nations in the world today are represented by a compilation of over 60 continuous conflicts both within a nation and between nations. The core source of the conflicts are based on religious and economic disagreements, as well, as the continuing phenomenon of autocratic rulers. This is why the name "United Nations" seems to be an inaccurate title. Pursuing true unity does not seem to be the ongoing actual intent. It is a classic example of the practice of claiming one thing, goal-wise, but not in actual action.

## Taking a Closer Look at the Individual in the Discussion of Unity

Being united as an individual is the foundation of any and all investigation and insight on the definition of unity. For the actual basis of understanding and soliciting the group unity is first founded on the understanding of the establishment of unity within the individual. As a person comes to maturity, it creates a realization that being one in the whole realization of what constitute mental and emotional well-being, promotes the balance and appreciation for all the cooperative workings of the body, and mind. It is especially apparent in the areas of sports when the parts of the body are aligned to to complete the various actions of participation in the game activities. Whether it is the pitcher focusing on the precision movements of all body parts to create a direct throw to the plate in a designated area above the plate, or the pole vaulter running and precisely placing the pole into the slot to bend the pole in such a way as to carry his body weight over the barrier and land appropriately on the designated padding, the individual sport's participant has got to have developed a holistic and totally united agreeing of all body parts and mind directive to accomplish the goal. In the area of mental pursuit of creating the story, essay, research paper or book, all aspects of a person's intelligent capacity is brought together in a most collaborative and collective manner to use all memory, investigative and summarizing capacities to organize sequence, progression, initiating proposal, filling in the steps and bringing the entirety of it to a reasonable and believable conclusion. In each case there is a clear and constant need for a unifying action for a final accomplishment.

All parts have to be declared, attended to, and used in a balanced and heightened manner to assure completion of the original intent. When the individual experiences the value and results of personal unity in one's actions, that creates a balance and a perspective that promotes their capacity and need to promote unity within any and all groupings of people.

A national Christian organization, "Christian Apologetics and Research Ministry," on its online internet site (Slick, p. 1-2) states the following regarding unity: "What is it that Unites Us? Primarily, it is the saving work of Jesus Christ that unites Us. Secondarily, it is the essential doctrines that define orthodoxy. We have, as a common heritage, the blood of Christ that has been shed for the forgiveness of our sins." This supports the fact that the unity of the faith that is advocated by the work of the Apostle Paul as stated in I Corinthians 12, makes it clear that the individual can only serve within the Body of Christ (the church) according to their giftedness by the power of the Spirit of God, as they yield to the salvation offered by God the Father in Jesus. Our yielded mind, heart and spirit enables a balance to control all our "parts" so that when we work within the church, we are already tuned in on the value and absolute critical nature of unity within the local congregation. Our individual unity within our own spirit, and mind enables us to cooperate and promote the unity that Jesus prayed for, as he was preparing for the eventual death by crucifixion. He was even repetitive of his admonition regarding the necessity for his return to the Father so that the Holy Spirit could be sent to unify the new Church of God, establishing the organization of the of the New Covenant. Where the Law had been the overall provision for unity under the Old Covenant, now the Holy Spirit within the spirit of the newly born-again believer was The means of unifying the individual to assure unity within the entirety of the Body of Christ, the church.

## Definitions of Unity within the Christian Faith

Jesus taught that Satan and the evil of sin has been beaten ... the war is won by the culminating work of Jesus at the cross and his resurrection. Christ's return to this Earth at His second-coming will not be the victory point, as that has already occurred. We are simply waiting for his return to begin the work of restoration and the completion of the Creation, as Paul the Apostle tells us in the letter to the Colossians, chapter one: "He is the image of the invisible God, the firstborn of all creation. For by Him all things were created, both in the heavens and on earth, visible and invisible, whether thrones or dominions or rulers or authorities— all things have been created through Him and for Him. He is before all things, and in Him all things hold together. He is also the Head of the Body, the church: and He is the beginning, the firstborn from the dead, so that He Himself will come to have first place in everything (verses 15-18). Paul concludes the declaration of Jesus' status and power by ending the chapter with the following: "We proclaim Him, admonishing every man and teaching every man with all wisdom, so that we may present every man complete in Christ. For this purpose, also I labor, striving according to His power, which mightily works within me" (verses 28-29). The defining of unity in Christ, is not just the overall effort to keep people working together in teams, congregations, denominations and in the universal church, it is founded and wholly dependent upon the work of Christ within the mind and heart of the individual Christian believer. As each Christian believer "works out his own salvation with fear and trembling" to mature in Christ, becoming, therefore, more and more like Him, each day the very nature of the oneness that Christ prayed for in the Gospel of John, chapter 17, for all believers is refined, developed and increased to an improving desire and empowerment to be in unity with not only God, but with each of God's children, or brothers and sisters in Christ's Body … the Church. So, we can see that unity is a result of maturing, growing up in the knowledge and wisdom of God, by the yielding to the Holy Spirit, the comforter and source of maturing power, and desiring to be more like Jesus each day.

Unity in our world is a matter of determination for the ultimate accomplishment of goals and projects for the completion and maintenance of efficiency, improvement and accomplishing goals. It is a critical factor in the success of any business, corporation or association. As the founders of these entities determine what it is that is to be done, they cooperatively develop procedures, protocols and actions that when followed will promote the accomplishment of the corporate goal. When the Roman empire was developing, it became obvious to those who originated the concept of a new empire that there would have to be standards by which the governance and productivity of the new empire would be guided. The promotion of victories for the accumulation of territory, for the acquisition of military prominence and the development of an economy that would provide the financial and productive power for its success had to be established and enforced throughout the territories. Continuing in the process of establishing the meaning of unity, we find that in the Merriam-Webster's Collegiate Dictionary (11th edition, p. 1368-1369) that unity is "An act or instance of uniting or joining two or more things into one, as 'the formation of a single political unit from two or more separate and independent units, a uniting in marriage, the growing together of separate parts [union]." Also, to define unity specifically, the definition states: "The quality or state of not being multiple: oneness, and "the quality or state of being made one: unification [unity]."

According to some of the more technical discussion on the topic of unity in the context of understanding the overall characteristics of nature as reviewed in the environment of philosophical theory, specifically the topic of geometric generalization (Durgun, p. 1). This theory "assumes that the physical reality is based on some a priori abstract principles (e.g. the principles of mathematics, geometry, logic, causality, unity, etc.), and it attempts To derive the physical existence as a natural result of these abstract principles. This derivation was discussed previously. These abstract principles do not have material bodies that can be directly observed. In fact, these principles can hardly be extracted from experiments, but they can be known through intuition ... the logical reasoning of the causality and unity is more problematic."

In most all sciences, in most all areas of research and investigation, there is a recognition of the factor of unity.

Another site online, "MacPhail's Manuscripts: Sermons" (MacPhail, p. 1-2), states: "The focus is on the nature of the unity we are called to. We are not called to a superficial kind of unity, it is not a calling to a handholding kind of unity, but it is a calling to a unity that mirrors the unity of the Trinity. This is what Jesus prayed for in John 17, praying that, '(the church) may be one, as (He and the Father) are one.' Paul proclaims, 'to God be the glory in the church.' Paul says that the worthy walk of the Christian must be done with 'all humility.' It takes a humble person to admit we do not have all the answers." An article from the Nashville Tennessean newspaper by a local pastor for the weekly Sunday commentary states, "What is primary? What is secondary? What really counts? That's what this scribe in Mark 12 is trying to figure out. He wants to know, what is the greatest priority in life. And Jesus answers him by saying that our lives should be focused on having a relationship with God and a relationship with others. And that it should happen in that order. So before we get wrapped up with doctrine, biblical liberalism, worship styles, social issues and church shopping, we should ask ourselves, 'How are we doing when it comes to following these two commandments? That will tell us a lot about our life and our faith (Stauffer, p. 6)." If the unity that Christ advocated and prayed for with such earnestness to the Father God is to be established, it must first be established in the hearts and minds of the individual believer. Again, it is clear that unity is a state that is contingent upon the infilling of the Holy Spirit at the time of new birth. Countering the carnal mind of self-indulgence and preoccupation with ones own personal needs in life, the mind of the Spirit invades the mind of the born-again believer and begins to unify with one's Lord and Savior as He was one with His Father God. That internal cleansing, healing and directive toward a life of love, faith and total Commitment to the work and word of God enables the individual to more effectively live in unity within the Body of Christ. In the Christianity Today article, "Why Unity is So Hard," the author states: "Christians value Jesus' prayer (John 17) ... that his followers may be as one, but, valuing Christian unity is not the same as realizing it" (Metzger,

p. 71). He goes on to say: "Individual personalities, faults, and sins are not The only factors [ed., 'that cause of contribute to disunity] ... Cleveland [the author whose book he is evaluating] does not discount substantive ideological and cultural differences or deny how hard it is to discard our various labels ... she agrees that principles and theological convictions are important." So it is a complicated thing to realize that unity must occur among the humans that make up the church.

One of the first things that happened to the early church, as described by the Apostle Paul, is such matters as individuals following an individual who is influential to their grasp of the faith. In the book of first Corinthians, Paul takes issue with some following various leaders/teachers to the separation of one group from the others. Right off, the the new believers of the Way, are beginning to distinguish themselves by the particular Christian leader they may have been originally taught the truths of Christ and the gospel. Paul takes immediate issue with this "immature" practice as being divisive. The mature in their relationship with God by accepting the salvation message focused on the life, death and resurrection of Jesus of Nazareth, recognize it all depends on one's relationship with Jesus, not another human leader.

As the book, "Undermining the Gospel: The Case for Church Discipline," addresses the tendency of Christians of a variety of biblical understanding making decisions regarding the interpretation of scripture, the point is made that this very characteristic over the many centuries of defining such matters as church unity and how it is to be practiced makes for disunity (Rogers, p. 17). He goes on to say, "How the pastor leads the church to regard the scriptural teaching on church discipline [ed., or any other doctrine] concerning incidents in the congregation will determine the fate of the church's spiritual fellowship and whether or not the church becomes complicitous with the world in undermining the gospel." In the NIV Bible Commentary, the statements about Eph. 4, and Paul's concern for the individual accountability for laying the foundation that supports Christian unity reflect the following: " …Paul turns from doctrinal concerns to practical ones. It must not be imagined, however, that the break is complete. Theology continues to be interwoven with the moral exhortations that make up the bulk of chapters 4-6. The apostle now specifies four graces that evidence this essential proportion between calling and character: humility, gentleness, patience, and forbearance. These are all qualities necessary for good relations with others. The absence of these qualities may jeopardize Christian unity. It is assumed that unity between Christians already exists as given in Christ by the Spirit. The one Spirit is the agent of unity … peace is the one clasp that ensures that this God-given unity will not fall apart" (Barker, p. 766-767). As is becoming more obvious, the essential element to the gaining of unity within the Body of Christ, whether on a worldwide scale or in the Local congregation, is the Spirit filled and yielded believer in the Gospel of Christ.

# CHAPTER TWO

## The Historical and Immediate Obstacles to Unity

As far as historical records go, there is evidence of human communities and human governments waging war and conflict against neighboring groups, communities and nations, usually with another form of government, and even variation on the basic autocratic rule as demonstrated in monarchies, kingdoms and empires throughout history. Whether one investigates the longest of empires, the one established by the Romans, or the ones that strove to establish themselves in the twentieth century (namely the Reichs of the Germans) which provoked World War I and II, in every case the method was based on conquest for the sake of their concept of unity. They wanted the world as they knew it, to be subjected to their rule, therefore, in their minds establishing a form of unity that subjugated everyone else to their ways of government, culture, religious belief, and life-style. It also included the forced dominance of their particular language and its forced learning in various ways.

In the modern world of the twenty-first century, now over a decade in existence, we have a world ... a planet ... filled with over 7,000 languages (not dialects or other variations on a particular language, but actually 7,000 distinct languages), and at last count, by the United Nations, one hundred and ninety-five nations. Each of those languages represents a separate historical development of the people who speak it. According to the Wycliffe Bible Translators, there is yet to be finally established the final count of languages, as such areas of the giant island of Borneo, have not been fully investigated for the distinguishing of what might be new and undiscovered languages. As the population of the Earth moves toward eight billion people, and the incredible impact of modern electronic instrumentation moves all people much closer together in most every way, making factual information available in ways hardly conceived of merely five decades ago, the actual distinctive characteristics of culture, religion, daily practices and will be confronted. Over one billion people are adherents to the Islamic religious beliefs and corresponding culture. Yet even within Islam, there are distinct groups of variant subgroups that are adamant about their interpretation of the Quran, or the book of their faith/religious beliefs. In other words, whether one selects Islam, Buddhism, or even Atheism, there will be schism, breakaways, and splinter groups, for a plethora of reasons. One significant example of Christian splinter groups, off an original denomination, is the Worldwide Church of God, now renamed the Grace Communion International. According to a variety of websites online, there are now "hundreds of splinter groups ..." that continue to split even further. This occurred back in the mid-1990's, after the death of it's founder, Herbert W. Armstrong (1986). As time progressed in the aftermath, eventually the new president began to oversee some changes in doctrinal beliefs, the primary one being the keeping of the Jewish Sabbath and the annual Holydays no longer. This created disunity on a pervasive scale across the world of local congregations in what had been the Worldwide Church of God. The question that is obviously asked is: "Why did this schism take place?" The answer is both simple and can have great complexities.

Upon contacting one of the groups that was formerly a part of the WCG under Herbert Armstong, the ultimate result was their response that defended their position that what they continued to do was what was originally taught all along by Mr. Armstrong. Since the schism occurred, they had simply continued to teach and proclaim the message as he always taught. It was the newly revised teachings of the second president (Joseph Tkach) that was incorrect. Of course, when inquiring of the newly formed and re-titled WCG as the Grace Communion International, as to the status of their continuance from the teachings under Herbert Armstrong, they carefully explain that the second president began to investigate the beliefs of Mr. Armstrong, and when further challenged by other New Testament scholars (specifically a Catholic priest scholar who presented a life-changing understanding of a key teaching/doctrine of the former WCG), Mr. Tkach began to check out other doctrines, which created a lengthy domino effect, changing a number doctrinal foundational beliefs to the point that they would eventually embrace evangelical Christianity. A recent contact with one of the larger splinter groups produced a letter of both clarification and an example of the issues that often describe the particulars of why groups end up breaking apart and why the groups themselves begin to set themselves up for further splinterings. The United Church of God, headquartered in Ohio, has managed to take on the characteristics and appearance of the original Worldwide Church of God under the presidency of its founder, Herbert W. Armstrong. They use, for example the same name for one of their identifiable publications (The Good News magazine). An interview with the individuals that were a part of the original WCG, and are now with the United Church of God, demonstrated their commitment to the "original truths" of the WCG as an indication of remaining unified with the basic Truths of their version of "true Christian dogma and associated beliefs of applying those doctrinal interpretations."

What is represented in this description of a recent splintering of a denomination is one that would be typical of any church group who comes to a point of having leaders, or members of a mutually agreed upon group within a congregation that need to confront the current leadership with the belief that current doctrine, practice or emphasis may need revision to a "more up-to-date set of beliefs." Often times, it can be something as simple as how many staff need to be salaried within a specific congregation that for, say, economic reasons, must consider dropping a position or two, to keep a financial balance. If a group within the congregation believe that too much money is being spent on salaries there can be reason in enough members to either relieve the pastor of duties, or go to the governing board and demand a change.

If one goes to the book of Acts of the Apostles, there are immediate examples to be found that show a basis for potential division and disunity. One prominent one is the complaints that certain cultural groups of widows were not being attended to like another group of widows (Acts 6). At the very beginning of the Way … the Church of the New Testament, even among the Jews who were converted to the New Covenant there was dissention due to alleged preference being shown to the native Jews over the widows in the Hellenistic Jews. This eventually was rectified by the Apostles delegating the resolution of the matter to newly ordained deacons, who would from that time one address the non-preaching/teaching aspects of "congregational" physical matters. This goes to exemplify the problem with issues of maturity in Christ, to which Paul the Apostle had to continually address, as most emphatically attended to in the two letters to the Corinthian church members. He did not end with Corinth issues, as there was the profound matter of Peter yielding to the group that tended toward demanding that the entire obligations of the Old Covenant remain a practice for all new Christians, even though many of the new converts were now non-Jews, or Gentiles. It was such an influence on Peter that Paul had to confront Peter with his showing deference to the "circumcision faction" (as described in Galatians 2) while attending to matters in the church at Antioch. For the early church, the truth that salvation was meant for all people, as frequently mentioned in the Old Testament prophecies, was apparently a very difficult idea to readily accept, as the focus had always been on the Israelites being the ones who would be restored with the coming of the Messiah. However, as Paul recognized, it was not a matter of what special race you belonged to, but a simple matter of accepting the message of the good news by faith.

As time went on, there were many other issues of disunity that were regularly being presented to the church leadership as it spread around the Mediterranean and out to even what is present day England and India. To what extent the church grew as the first century ended and the apostles either died due to age, or some form of persecuting acts by the Jews and the Roman empire representatives, is a matter of historical record both by Christian scholar research or general research of parallel documents, generic histories outside the Christian faith, as governments of many nations dealt with new religions. A text on the book of Romans makes the following statements regarding the issue of unity as described by the Apostle Paul: "Paul's intention to persuade his Judean and Greek addressees of the significance of what (I later argue) is a new identity derived from the righteousness of God through faith in Christ is evident in the verses that frame the passage under consideration (Rom. 1: 17, 3:21). Yet although the goal might be to include all within a new in-group identity, modern research has shown how the original group of memberships of those whom it is hoped can be brought together can seriously interfere with the process of re-categorization. It appears that if the participants feel their viability and distinctiveness, as result, that will exacerbate any bias they feel and exhibit toward members of the other (sub) group. I submit that in seeking to re-categorize

Judeans and Greeks into a new group in Christ, or to bring to them forcefully the meaning of having been so re-categorized, Paul faced precisely this problem in subgroup loyalties. We have seen that Paul's experience in Galatia had probably taught him to be more sensitive to subgroup identities (Esler, p. 143).

Clearly the work of the apostles ran into the issues of group identity almost immediately. They had to help the Judeans (native Israel citizens, even though dominated by their Roman governors) who identified themselves even more emphatically as the chosen ones of the God of Israel, deal with the sudden influx and infiltration of Gentiles. People, who for the most part were completely oblivious to the history of Israel and the Old Covenant and its written word and its clear dictations of how to conduct one's life as a "righteous" Israelite. As time went on, many other reasons for distinctions developed. Just the fact that towns, villages, cities and other settlements were often quite distanced from the ones around them, despite well established Roman roads, caused Christian groups to develop over time in a unique manner entwined with the local culture in general and the issues of language.

Certainly there are numerous additional reasons for almost unintentional changes in the conduct and application of the beliefs of the New Covenant key doctrinal issues. How one reaches out the rest of humanity in each culture would become a protocol specific to the that nation, culture or even ethnic groups. Consider the fact of so many languages where the translating of certain words and/or concepts would be genuinely "foreign" to a group that has not been informed about something mentioned in the Bible, but not a part of their experience or their natural environment, created differences. For example, the Aleutes of "fartherest north" North America, better known as Alaskan or Yukon natives, have hundreds of words for snow and ice that are very specific to their daily and annual issues of weather and searching for the foods of that area of the world. For them the idea of a castle or temple would be most difficult to understand. Explaining the intimacies of the Mosaic laws of daily conduct would be even more complex and confusing. Yet, vice versa, to the average Judean, the snow defining words of the Aleutes would be as confusing and complex.

When one applies the basics of how to meet as a Christian community in both contexts so that the Christian can learn the essentials of getting along with one's brother or sister in the Lord, becomes difficult as the Alaskan native new believing woman tries to accept the fact that in Christ she is at the same level of value as any man. Being ostracized from one small Aleut group over a basic Christian value has quite different impact and complications as it would in a place of reasonable climate and varieties of people groups already as a part of the local community.

By the time the Roman Catholic Church and the Eastern Orthodox Church becomes rooted in their geographic areas (and for that matter the Coptic branches of Christian believers), the entrenched differences are basically taken for granted as the "Way" in their geographical locations. The average person's ability to read the scriptures, much less have access to the Bible to read for themselves creates another long-term over the centuries phenomenon that seems so hard to accept in today's world. But the fact of the average believer becoming totally dependent upon the very few who could read and teach the contents of Bible truth was the basic reality until the times of the Reformation … or Protestant revolution away from top down religious autonomy to the promotion of the individual believer learning the truth of Christ in their own community under the auspices of ministers of the faith as the new evangelists. The rest of the issues of historical impacts on the unity of the faith will be addressed more specifically in the chapters to come.

# CHAPTER THREE

# A Review of Christian Literature as to Issues of Unity in Recent Times

The intensity of disunity, and on the other hand, unity in the Christian faith, as of the past half century can be readily described with the following example statements taken from a letter from a correspondence representative of a "cult" labeled group within the overall grouping of today's Christian realm. The author was responding to an inquiry of a researching author, trying to gain insight into the characteristics of unity and disunifying factors. Among statements of deepest, serious concern for the correspondence author regarding the one wrote to him, is the following:

> "I read the introduction and conclusion of your book about Eternity ... a conclusion that says, 'there is no conclusion!' I agree with your statement that we should live by Romans 10:9-13. But you make it sound like we don't need to bother to walk in the steps of Jesus Christ. We are instructed to 'live by every word of God.' (Lk. 4:4) I'm confident that your book gives some nuggets

of truth ... However, I fear that you are being used by the god of this world to help delude people into a cheap grace, a false sense of security and a false conversion." (Hooser, p. 2)

Obviously the concerns of the "cult" representative were serious and sincere. It was a matter that justified the representative to take no qualms about labeling the beliefs of the author of the book as off the acceptable doctrine being addressed. It was doctrinally unacceptable to the point that the representative felt justified judging the veracity of the author of the book's relationship with God. There is no question that people who take a particular stance on any doctrinal issue are sincere and taking a position that they feel gives a protective wall to their belief. The Bible is replete with examples of individuals who came to a realization that their position was wrong and repented due to an experience of spiritual guidance/mentoring or insight, or did not. A prime example is the premier story of Adam and Eve, and their decision after making a fundamentally wrong choice about Satan's deceit, and later on the situation of Abraham telling a local king that his wife was his sister to avoid personal fear of being abused. There are other examples of people starting off making righteous and godly decisions with God's blessing, but ending up in a position far from where God had hoped they would be at the end of their life. A prime example is that of Solomon. Starting by using the gift of wisdom for the benefit of not only Israel, but for many from surrounding nations, such as the Queen of Sheba. But, as he began to "investigate" his world with the untold riches of the kingdom God had blessed him with, he managed to end up with all kinds of wives and not so productive international ties with wrongly influencing nations and cultures. In their book, "Break Down the Walls," Washington and Kehrein address the current issues of unity and lack of it. They state in the first unit of their book (Eight Biblical Principles for Reconciliation and Unity ... etc.) that, "Jesus tells us to carry his message to the lost world. We can start by intentionally worshipping with diverse groups of believers. Jesus wants us to be in unity, as a family. Unity is critical to the redemptive work of the Church. Our unity comes from a common relationship with Jesus Christ ... and it is only successful by the Holy Spirit bringing us together ... Christ's spirit in each of us. Pride is the primary source of racism, sectarianism and other forms of Disunity in Christ's disciples" (Washington, p. 15).

A recent journal acticle (Watts, p. 20), speaks to the issue of what a larger denomination or national organization within the realm of Christian organizations wants to see occur in the name of unity. The author states, "A lack of unity discredits the witness and work of the church for the world. This truth has long been emphasized by those concerned for the oneness of church ... the church's sanction of war and the participation of its members, in various forms of violence is the most glaring and harmful expression of disunity ... [ed. He goes on to cite the World Council of Churches constitution for the purpose of gaining unity through the common life in Christ ... the First Assembly of World Council of Churches proclaimed, "We are one in proclaiming to all (that war) is contrary to the will of God."] (Watts, Craig M., no. 3-4).

As can be readily seen at this point, the more modern issues of war and its related aspects can be, and is, a matter of great disagreement between major denominations. Why a group of people in today's world in the modern western world would take an anti-war position is certainly not a minor issue.

## Typical Problems in the Church Universal

Any religious section of a local newspaper will often have a Sunday message from one of the pastors of a recognized area church congregation. It is not uncommon for the theme to address a current matter in the news. Whether it be the war in Afghanistan, recent rashes of gang rapes, or the need for more cooperation to attend to the needy/homeless population, the pastor will give a particular bent to the message that reflects the denominational opinion, and even the willingness to contribute to the resolution of the community matter. Local congregations are often addressing issues of new construction/relocation. As communities populations change, whether the influx of immigrants, legal or otherwise, there can be conflicting presentations from denominations that create a confused understanding of the Christian beliefs on current matters. So, one church advocates taking in the immigrants to assist with their economic needs, with a clear message that it is not their responsibility to determine their legality as to immigration papers ... green cards ... processing for citizenship. Another church takes a clear position that states that obedience to US law is just as important for Christians as being helpful to the needy (illegal) immigrants. When one hears of new converts to Christianity in areas of the world today, for the most part associated with a majority Islamic culture, there are rather drastic and life-threatening situations developing and it is often reported that anti-Christian groups both threaten and kill converts. When the message goes out in the press to conjure up response and rectifying the situation, the Christian church needs to be in unity to immediately instigate action to bring safety and protection to those threatened. Even the governments that one would expect to execute action to protect the threatened Christians, have become almost defenseless, due to international policies of non-interference. When the many groups of Christian believers around the world have not unified protocol to address such matters, one has to wonder to what extent is the Church Universal actually united.

According to one research text on eldership in the Bible,

"Conflict among elders is a serious, all-to-common problem. It is appalling how little regard some Christian leaders have for the sacredness of the unity of the Body of Christ, and how quickly they will divide the body in order to gain their own way. In the end they may get their own way, but it is not God's way. The solution to the problem, however, is not to revert to one man's rule or to leave the church. That is the easy way out. The Christian solution is to humble oneself, love as Christ loved, wash one another's feet, repent, submit, pray, turn from pride, shun impatience, and honor and love one another ... that is the kind of leadership God wants elders to exemplify for His people." (Strauch, p. 96). Not even 90 years ago, even here in the advanced economy of the United States, it would have taken at least a week or so to contact someone in the central headquarters of most any Christian group/denomination to request counsel or assistance with a congregational internal matter of conflict. Phone calls were expensive and not very available.

Any postal communication would have taken weeks. The current economic and complex technological environment, making almost every item of interest immediately available to not only the one's intended to be informed/impacted/influenced, is on a phenomenal level and degree of impact from anyone's previous understanding. Keeping issues discreet and internal has become extremely difficult. Just a person going into a pastor's office for counsel can be shown by cell phone camera off to "you.tube" in a matter of minutes. Deriving implication and creating preliminary (never intended) judgments are indelibly influencing opinion and decisions, by what is referred to in today's western informational culture as a "shallow clientele." Too often the average believer within the Christian world has a minimal level of understanding of the teachings of the Bible. There is even less understanding for the average Christian believer as to the doctrinal teachings not only across various groups, but even that of their own Christian group/denomination. Shawn Grimsley in a short article on "Unity of Command in Management" as practiced across corporations, military, governmental agencies and business in general, notes the pervasiveness of this principle in modern business and organizations. It has become a significant factor in how most churches/denominational groups are managed. As seminaries and denominational colleges have emerged, they too have sought general certification just as most colleges and universities have to give value to the completed training and degree programs. As a result, the teachings on corporate management have impacted the manner in which the seminary professors discuss the management of the local church. One would think this would be a significant value, a protocol for management that has been proven as effective and profitable. The basic issue is … does it follow the guidelines and principles of the Bible? Are we to be organized as the Church Universal, or the local congregation, as if we are no different that the businesses of any current world culture/nation? (Grimsley, p. 1). In most cases within the Christian groups of the United States, such obligations as annual Internal Revenue Service declarations, create a heightened awareness of financial matters. Our unity in too many respects, although certainly acceptable and required by state and federal law, is promoted by the demands of our laws, culture and business standards. In other words, the unity one finds within the local church, across a denomination, or over a national association, is often fostered by the required standards of the legal requirements (highly so with respect to financial matters) for how an organization conducts its activities, its impact on "consumers/customers/ members" and the general daily practices of serving within the environment of business across the board. The current tendency in our modern world for Christian groups to continue to develop practices, protocols in worship and proposed new perspectives on the meaning of scripture from a doctrinal variant is not a new tendency in Christian belief reviews. In the text on Faith Founded on Fact, in chapter seven, the author presents just one example in particular of the need to clarify the Lutheran (based on the original segregating work of Martin Luther from the Roman Catholic church as a key empowerment), where it is stated, "But did these Lutheran apologists not inevitably weaken the biblical picture of man's total depravity, deemphasize the scriptural teaching concerning the Holy Spirit's work in salvation, and introduce a subtle synergism into the preaching of the gospel of divine grace?" (Montgomery, p. 149). The author goes on to disagree, and show that the critics are promoting heresy. So, the current context/environment within the Church Universal, which seems to promote, often unintentionally, is not new. Leaders take issue with other leaders in the name of retaining status, giving a merchandizing and promotional strategy of advertisement, whether intended or not, so that the legitimacy of their perspective/doctrine/teaching retains credibility. We do it today using the protocols and procedures taught in the universities/ colleges/seminaries that promote the accepted strategies of good business practice.

## Not so Typical Problems and Impact on the Church Universal

There are problems that have surfaced in the everyday promotion of the work of reaching out to the world with the message of the gospel. In this twenty-first century the immediate impact of members becoming involved in various forms of jealousy is rather convoluted and minimized. When one member sees another member, or one organized group sees another organized group, gain an advantage, there is room for subtle forms of jealous response. Why was our congregation not interviewed by the local news station regarding the impact of giving generously to the poor and disadvantaged in our community? This can become an ongoing issue in the local ministerial association. Where once these kind of matters got little or no wide-spread attention, now it is a really inexpensive way for the particular church group to advertize and gain an advantage in the numbers of new attendees and potential membership.

Another not so obvious twenty-first century matter that has significant impact on the promotion of unity is the fact that advertizing and promotion of the local congregation in the immediate community has become rather impacted by the protocols of any and all business practices. It is much more likely to return a response of new attendees by sending out flyers inviting local community members via US Mail than by individual congregation people extending personal invitations on a one-to-one basis … so the finance committee invests in the US Mail advertizing to gain more bang for the buck. Obviously, these matters of subtle use, some would insist that it is just a smarter strategy, are not going to be addressed in Christian journal articles, as they would create "unnecessary" backlash from pastoral associations. One might even say that it would be quickly blown off as a needless undermining of the efforts to spread the gospel in different times and advanced technological worlds. Pastor James Frease of Joy Church International, in Mount Juliet, Tennessee, insists that there is a huge difference between the strategies of today to reach people with the gospel. He states regularly at the beginning of church services, as an introductory statement for the benefit of new attendees, that there is a huge difference between being in unity and being in union. "The local congregation is going to be made up of people from all walks of life, and many cultures and even races in a non/cross-denominational church. It is more important to emphasize what we do agree on, and maintain a standard of disagreeing agreeably on the many peripheral matters within Christian circles than to waste precious time on secondary issues. As long as we agree that the only way to salvation is through God's grace and forgiveness as a direct action on His part by his love through faith in the Work of Jesus Christ's sacrifice and resurrection, the rest can be attended to over time. We persist in an environment of acceptance and agreeable dialogue with genuine desire to be in union to accomplish God's work in His Kingdom. (Frease, James. Sermon series on being one in Christ, 2006-2014).

Whereas, over the twenty centuries of the work of the Church Universal to reach the lost with the Gospel of Jesus Christ, God's ministry has attempted to present the genuine message, due to huge distances between Christian groups, and the local cultural influences, that simply distinguished Greek heritage from Roman heritage, the church stayed fairly static. But as the inventions of the past four centuries, and the extensive migration of people increased to new lands, it became more obvious that the ways of the local church members did not always match the traditions that had carried them in their previous locales (such as European nations, and African nations or colonies). In "Biblical Principles of the Unity of the Church," the editor notes in the fourth reason for unity, "In the New Testament this teaching of unity of the people of God is sustained (Eph. 2: 11-22, 4: 1-16). Yet the situation is different. No longer are the people of God circumscribed by ethnic, political, or geographical boundaries. All nations are to be discipled." Through the remarkable advancements in industry, science, inventions, communication and the increasing (on a logarithmic scale) of them, the whole process to proclaiming the gospel has become a great deal more complex. The message is the same, but the means to that end of proclaiming continually is being changed ... often with little or minimal review by the church universal as to the long-term and immediate impact of the affect on those being sought (Editor, p. 1-2).

With regard to the issues of eschatology, and the whole issue of when Christ is coming back, as a very provocative and continually addressed issue in our remarkable times, in his book, "Invasion of Other Gods: The Seduction of New Age Spirituality," David Jeremiah, a longstanding pastor and remarkably successful television evangelist/teacher, tells us: "No! This is a great time to be alive! We are privileged to be a part of a generation that can see the prophetic scenario that foreshadows end-time events. But only a fool would stand before his congregation or write a book and say, 'I am preaching that this is the final age … ' (he adds, ed.) Jesus also said there would be a generation which would see all the signs unfold that would signal His soon return. One evidence would be a one-world government joined with a unified religious system. Both are on the horizon today." (Jeremiah, p. 191) There are certainly a variety of responses from respected and notorious/ and non-notorious Christian leaders that would take issue with Dr. Jeremiah's interpretation of passages from the gospels like Mk. 13: 31-33. Our times for the promotion of the Church Universal and its message of Christ's message and His return are becoming more varied, promotional and complicated from the perspective of the ones to which the church is proclaiming this gospel. Instantaneous accessibility to any evangelist, proclaimer, leader representing their particular denomination or their own cross-denominational group, has become possible for most anyone, anywhere on the planet Earth. Never before has the availability of communication devices made the message of the gospel so extensively and pervasively accessible. However, the basic message comes across in so many and varied presentations. As a curious person in the nation of Nepal or Terra del Fuego scans his I-5 cell phone for internet Christian presenters, he runs into an A to Z library of possibilities. Remarkably there is no one to provide bottom-line advisory as to which is going the provide the best presentation of the Good News.

## Attempts to Rectify those Problems that Undermine Unity

With the organization of many denominations under the current National Association of Evangelicals and the National Council of

Churches represent a large scale effort across many denominations that have been a part of the Christian establishment over many years. These two associations represent a major portion of adherents to the Christian belief. The National Council of Churches is also related to similar associations across the 195 nations on the planet. These are efforts on the larger perspective to foster unity throughout Christendom. There are a number of authors from across all denominations that have attempted to promote unity through the production of books that focus on the value, reason, and biblical basis for searching for unity in all levels and environments of Christian groups. The author of "Every Teaching of Jesus in the Bible" clarifies from his perspective the basic effort to promote unity. He states, "Prayer that all believers might be one (Jn. 17: 20-23) … undoubtedly the misunderstood element of Jesus' prayer. Many people have viewed it as a call to organizational unity. Many sermons have been preached and many well-intentioned movements have been launched based on a misinterpretation of these verses … Jesus asked that the disciples might be one, 'as You, Father, are in Me, and I in You.' The unity of which Jesus spoke is organic. It is a unity which believers can have with the Lord, not with one another. The oneness is clearly defined in the text. What Christ described here is a mutual indwelling, patterned on the relationship with God that Jesus experienced during his life on earth. The outcome of a life lived in such intimate relationship with God is that Jesus will be seen in us, a witness to the world that God truly sent Jesus. It's not enough for others to hear about Jesus. They need to see Jesus in us. As we live in union with our Lord, God's glory will be on display." (Richards, p. 205-206)

Needless to say, for those within the realm of Christian belief, the efforts of Satan and his demons to deceive and undermine the efforts of promoting unity within the church are especially notorious and continually threatening. The Bible tells us he is the "father of lies." (Jn. 8:44) So the subject of unity within the church is going to be overly attended to by the devil and his promoters.

That is why we are admonished to walk in the Spirit and not in the flesh. (Rom. 8) Taking a Superficial approach to what needs to happen, strategy and priority-wise by God's people and the leaders of the church, to foster and establish unity, will leave each group and each leader open to ungodly influences. So, this is not just a matter of getting out there and bringing people together with any successful business and/or corporate efforts and strategies. It must be a process of genuine, sincere, humble and love-based prayerful investigation of what the Bible states brings unity to the Body of Christ. After all, the Bible states that the church of God is in fact, the Body of Christ.

So, the efforts to organize in order to reach out to all the groups of Christian believers, using as an example, the United States of America only, has brought about, as listed above, the National Council of Churches, and also, the National Association of Evangelicals. Ironically, at least at this point in the overall effort, has produced two major associations, who for all practical purposes, have created a proverbial "line in the sand," as to one groups distinguishing definitive beliefs and priorities versus the other's. In other words, each of their sub-groups, or denominations, had to be reviewed as to their beliefs before being allowed to enter the national association. The other way to look at it, is that each denomination looked to see what the defining beliefs were of the national association before they decided to even apply to it. In one respect, it is much the same situation as the national main political organizations: Democrats versus Republicans. Any person or smaller grouping of political interests would certainly give careful consideration before associating with one or the other … and, the national political association would be very attentive to the political advocacies and beliefs of the applying group.

From what can be seen so far, as we have reviewed the

background, biblical references, and current issues of unity in just the United States alone, it would appear that the effort for unity, as Christ defined it, has become more complicated, more a matter for greater investigation than one could have anticipated. Defining what Jesus meant, what Paul the Apostle and other writers of the New Testament went on to elaborate and/or clarify, takes us into territory that has been genuinely and exhaustively referenced in many Christian documents: individually authored books, manuals of each denomination (or at least often addressed in the literature produced by each Christian group offering such discourse, definition), and extensive and respected commentaries on the Bible. Two thousand years of advancing the proclamation of the Gospel of Jesus Christ has produced so many groups of Christian believers who developed into what they are today, as a result of geography (distance and isolational issues), culture, language and tradition. With over 7,000 languages (NumberOf. net, p. 1), and 195 nations (many of which, as is true in India, have a multiplicity of languages and sub-Cultures) (WorldAtlas.com, p. 1) the matter of bringing all Christians together in whatever sense is meant by unity at this point seems like a overwhelming work for the Universal Church.

# CHAPTER FOUR

# Issues of Disunity within Humanity in General

## Cultural Issues

Our world is terribly complex today ... yet many issues that exist today are merely "updated" versions of issues that have plagued humanity from the very beginning. Genesis, chapter four, of the Old Testament describes the first murder ... brother killing brother. The point for those searching for the keys and principles/strategies for church unity is that the reason why unity is so difficult to nurture in any culture, much less across cultures, is that differences, even on an individual level can foster resentment, feelings of being segregated or left out of the current activities, and result in thoughtless, emotional response. Often the response, the reaction to the the alleged slight, is merely a group fostered prepared reaction to any perceived discrimination. Dr. Ben Carson, a possible U.S. presidential candidate, believes that the nation has long needed a common vision ... since the conclusion of the Civil War, which promoted radical change and a much needed commitment to unity (Carson, p. 174-175).

Stepping back for a moment in this line of description in

the context of human relations, one can compare to the typical baseball team. There are nine players on the team: three in the outfield, five in the infield and a pitcher. Although they comprise a team (compare to a nation, state, community or specific religion), with team goals and cooperative strategies to assure a winning continuing practice in any game, each player develops personal expertise that enables him or her to exceed in that positional role. So each is focused on two things: personal acclaim for contribution to the win, and cooperative contribution for the exercise of melding the work of all to maximize the chances for the team's success. So although each culture exists for the most part in a particular nation, geographical area, or established community, each member of the culture has their own personal desired goals and beneficial accomplishments within that culture. In the book, "Faith Founded on Fact," the reference is made to the effort of Muhammad Ali to defend his "cultural/religious" choice in Islam versus the beliefs of Christianity. (Montgomery, p. 97) The author explains that such confrontations are based on the personal understanding of the cultural choice's facts and apologetics, and that no matter how well presented and argued, it ultimately comes to that person's faith and trust in what he has come to believe is the proofs of his groups cultural establishment. So the Lutheran will come to a particular, self-established, based on personal grasp and acceptance of what constitutes that Christian cultural groups basis for distinguished existence, in their tolerance for fellowship with someone of any other Christian group (Episcopal, Roman Catholic, Southern Baptist, or cross-denominational). Needless to say, just the statement of where one attends church services will immediately set up a set of barriers in the mind of both individuals, or each denominational group versus the other. Culture is more than simply a racial or physiological appearance (such as distinguishing characteristics of face and skin color or tone). There are clearly instances even within the nations of the continent of Africa, where the people of one tribe make a total draw-in-the-line set of distinctions resulting in total segregation from a tribe not all that far away, neighboring them. To them, there is no similarity at all between them and the other tribe people, yet an outsider/foreigner will see no distinctions at all, except for the style of clothing or some religious variations. For one of their tribe (culture) to separate and take on the culture of another group would be considered heresy in the strongest terms, even to the point of ostracizing to extremes. There is a recent article about a New York Times writer [a black American] who was asked about the ongoing situation with young people joining gangs and using guns to gain personal and gang notoriety who responded with: " ...to often people take the Bible and use it to support their particular existing viewpoint (Luo, p. 53). Too often the need to belong to a particular group (whether from birth or choice) creates the attitude of the individual and his or her group that segregates them from others. A text entitled, Explore the Book, gave this rendering of the meaning of Ephesians 3-4 of the New Testament: " ...and that during the present age an elect people, the Church, should be gathered out, irrespective of nationality—an elect people who should be brought collectively into an intimate union of life and love and eternal glory with him." (Baxter, p. 176) Another perspective on cultural impact, is made by a set of authors who write of the historical tendencies and impact of urbanization of people across all nations and groups. One states, " ...throughout its early period, Christianity seems to have been most appealing precisely to those marginal groups that were not engaged in landholding in agricultural production, or in service of rulers ... in brief, Christianity has been linked from its inception to urbanized people involved in producing and trading ... corporations have created more wealth than most of humankind can imagine." This gives us an extended picture of the development of Christianity. It is not a belief that has evenly developed across all groups of people since it was established by the teaching of Jesus in the area of Jerusalem. Paul the Apostle and the other leaders of the Way, expanded its awareness in the areas of where groups of Jews (or Judeans as is more commonly referred to by scholars today), namely urban areas. Even as Paul was finally making his way to Rome, the described journey took him from Jerusalem through a number of cities as listed in Acts of the Apostles (Boulton, p.305).

## Racial Issues

As described above, the initial racial environment of Christian believers was within the group known as Jews. They were the inhabitants of the area known as Judea, which was under the rule of the Roman Empire at the time of Christianity's beginning. There is a remarkable story of an instance for renowned historical individual of Jewish background who was one of the many prisoners in Nazi camps during World War II, who eventually survived to tell of actually meeting a former Nazi guard after one of her presentations, and how she has to overcome the natural desire to deny his conversion, simply because he was one who caused her sister' death in that camp ... 'how could God allow him to be converted and forgiven, much more making me as a converted Jew forgive him' (Yancey, p. 274). All groups have had their times of non-acceptance of another group, whether a racial issue or otherwise. The racial issues seem to have been the most critical, impacting and divisive. Here in the United States, the 1965 Civil Rights Act, represents just one giant step to overcome the long-standing denigration of African born and ancestored United States citizens. Even to this date there are many churches within the US that are basically segregated, either all black or all white, or often, anymore, all Hispanic or all Asian (Korean, Chinese, Japanese although not as common). Often this is due to the tendency for ethnic/cultural groups to chose to locate in areas of urban environments where others of their group (race, ethnicity, culture) have already established a locale within that city. Some would say this gives legitimacy to the observation by Boulton earlier.

Jesus, himself, established the beginnings, or foundation of the "get past the racial issues," when He sat down a well in Samaria, needing a drink of water. In the old text "The Gospel Primer," it reads as follows: "In this valley was the city of Sychar, and outside the gates of the city was a well, called the well of Jacob. Jesus, being weary and footsore, sat down by the well to rest … as he sat by the well, a woman of Samaria came to draw water … she ignored Jesus as he was a Jew … but Jesus asked for a drink … she asked why he spoke to her, since they (Jews and Samaritans) did not communicate at all. [Jesus' response was one of the first indications of the fact that the gospel was not just for Jews, but for the whole world.] He said, 'If you knew the gift of God, and who it was that says to you, 'Give me drink,' you would have asked of him, and he would have given to you living water.'" Of course, the implications were not obvious as she was to become enamored with his ability to know all about her. And she went on to effectively pass the words of Jesus on to her whole community. The significance lies in the fact that Jesus even bothered at all, breaking through racial, cultural and ethnic, national boundaries even under the fact of Roman rule. Yet we see the new Body of Christ in Acts 4, as a group of united and wholly cooperative people: "Now the large group of those who believed were of one heart and mind, and no one said that any of his possessions was his own, but instead they held everything in common." (Acts 4: 32, p. 1868, Holman Christian Standard Bible). Here we see that as the Church began there was a empowering spirit through the Spirit of God to join in all facets of life with one another as brothers and sisters in the family of God … with God as the Father, and Jesus as the Son. Whether they had to speak of unity or togetherness during this post Pentecost consolidation time was not indicated, but the writing of Luke who is the author of Acts, shows that the actual actions, behaviors and demonstration of the hearts and minds of the converted Jews who were now followers of the Way, showed no other signs. This would be the basis for all that Paul had to write in the book of Romans 9, as he poured out his heart as to his hopes of the people of Israel (Jews, Judeans) as the original descendents of Abraham and how as Christians were seeing God take in non-Jews as believers regardless of actual ancestry. Before God, race was no longer the issue … only faith in the work of Jesus Christ. (White, p. 113)

## Governmental Issues

Probably the most remarkable instance of government becoming a part of the life of those who believed in Jesus, was the instance of Peter the Apostle being impacted by a vision as he was enjoying a break with a friend in Joppa. As he was waiting for a meal being prepared he fell into a trance (Acts 10: 10) and was confronted with a direct contradiction of what foods were lawful to eat as listed in the Old Testament book of Leviticus (chapter 11). In fact, Peter was being told by God in the vision through the angel representative that all foods were now okay for consumption: "What God has cleansed, no longer consider unholy." Stepping back from this immediate experience for Peter, about to enjoy a noon meal, we strive to gain a true sense of just how impacting this was for him. For him to hear from anyone that it is okay to eat just anything someone gives to you, regardless of its content, how it was prepared, and what animals are involved was not only a profound contradiction to all he knew and lived by all his life, but was in direct disobedience to the word of God as he has heard and read throughout his life as a Jew. Now a vision from God himself tells Peter to make a huge change.

Within a few minutes the representatives of a centurion (Roman high-level officer) comes to tell Peter that their officer has had a vision as well telling him to contact Peter. All of a sudden it dawns on Peter that something bigger than what you can and cannot eat is going on … so he soon heads to the location of where the Centurion lives. Again, the early church leader is being confronted with the larger picture of God's great purpose for mankind. Eventually they are able to discuss their own interplay with God's angel and realize that God's plan is for all people, regardless of race, culture and background, to be participants in God's salvation.

Even here in the United States of America, the issues of race continue to be a matter of national and local urban issues. An example of how a group of people from eastern Europe came to the United States and retained their own unity … unity of culture, language and race is the "Evangelical Unity of Czech-Moravian Brethren in North America." (Mead, p. 175-176) This group have made a special effort to retain their culture, racial distinctions and separation from the larger culture of the United States. Even though they are more often United States citizens, their basic foundational beliefs and support for their decisions as a church group are primarily not based on United States founding principles, but those of the nation they originated from. Of the 195 nations on our planet, in each and every case, there is an origination primarily based on a particular race, culture, sub-culture or ethnicity. The national interests and history of each nation developed out of that race, culture or ethnicity. So even though today, most nations are impacted on an international level, whether a simple focus on accommodating visitors and tourists, or being a massively influential nation, like the United States, Russia, China or India. Most all races and cultures, except for extreme examples as in the Amazon Jungle areas of east Brazil or the island of Borneo, have interplayed with other nations and their cultures. Periodicals, like National Geographic magazine, have provided increased distribution of the specifics of peoples and their racial qualities, their long-held beliefs or culture and religion for over a hundred years. The international computer internet with all of its facets, has created a world, integrated relational contact, that allows contact across all nations, governmental issues, and even military conflicts.

## Financial Issues

One of the greatest matters of money and the impact on the local church over the history of Christianity is the determination of how all the ministries are to be funded. Many denominations are absolutely convinced that the "doctrine of tithing" is a continuous stream of expectation and essential source of financing the presentation of the Gospel message. There are those in many denominations that consider tithing a matter of Old Testament command and not related to the New Testament as emphasized in the book of Hebrews (chapter 8, verse 13). The other issues of finance relate to the commonality, at least in the western world, of corporate procedure and policy, as it relates to government oversight. Most United States churches are heavily influenced by corporate practice and the demands of federal and state finance laws. It all began long ago. "Biblical scholar, Dr. Richard Halverson, has said, 'When the Greeks got the gospel, they turned it into a philosophy; when the Romans got it, they turned it into a government; when the Europeans got it, they turned it into a culture, and when the Americans got it, they turned it into a business' ... here are some not-so-discreet differences between corporate processes and spiritual processes ... 1. Business casts a vision of what it wants to accomplish and then sets out to gather resources ... 2. Business starts with incorporating documents to guide them ... the church only uses them to comply with public governing agencies." (Coffee, p. 1 of 3).

## Generic Issues that May Not be Obvious

Believe it or not there are aspects life on our planet that impact us in the most apparently coverted ways. One example is the influence of the national and state lotteries that are a constant presence in most small grocery or gasoline side-stores. These winnings are a constant hope for so many Americans in the middle income and low-income groups. It is not uncommon for those who attend the local Christian denominational group/church congregation to, from time to time, purchase a lottery ticket ... just for fun, mind you. In other words, as a simple, but impacting example of how the culture around the average Christian, especially in our modern western societies, getting into practices like taking a chance on winning a gambling pot of money, can distract from Bible teaching, and take one away from the core of the Gospel and more toward the practices and standards of the local society. After all, if the culture looks at betting one's money on the possibilities of winning a grand prize as just a fun recreational activity with no moral implications, what keeps the Christian believer from falling prey? This small issue, relative to the core beliefs of the Gospel of Jesus Christ, can become such a matter of concern, that a person could be asked to "leave the fellowship" if your public life does not reflect the beliefs of the rest of the local group of believers. In other words, it would be a matter that causes the majority to feel keeping the person within the group of believers would be a disunifying acceptance.

On the other hand, there can be an issue that simply is not to be addressed, basically ignored and treated as irrelevant in order to maintain peace and keep the façade of unity going. In the text, "Congregations in Conflict," the following is described regarding a not so uncommon tendency: "If families have homes, families also avoid politics and other controversial issues, or at least middle-class families do ... implying that groups (in this case, congregations) with a close family-like attachment suppress disagreement and avoid debate ... one pastor found out how difficult it was to spark public discussion of social issues in his 'family' congregation ... when asked what his congregation's position was on abortion or homosexuality, they reported no official stand" (Becker, p. 87). So we see an effort to avoid conflict, to promote unity, but based on not being real, involved and striving to establish and reinforce standards of Christian core values. Unity is not to be trivialized through ignoring reality.

# CHAPTER FIVE

# The Example of Christ in the New Testament

Ultimately, Christianity is wholly and completely based on the Word of God, the Bible as found explained in the New Testament. One scholar of the New Testament tells us, "(regarding exegesis of N. T. writings) Read the entire document through in English in one sitting ... there is no substitute for this step. You never start exegeting a book at chapter 1, verse 1. The first step always is to read the entire document through before analyzing any of its parts, and you gain such a sense by reading it through." (Fee: No. 1, p. 34) We can certainly understand such advise, as one would never handle the items at a crime scene until the entire room, area or location is seen from all views and perspectives as a whole. It is only then that the individual items in the crime scene are then examined for their relevance to the determination of what it all provides as evidence. When one reads the entirety of what Jesus taught, we are compelled to read through each of the Gospels, and even a line or two from such texts as the Acts of the Apostles were Paul quotes a statement of Jesus ... "It is better to give than receive." (Acts 20:35)

Next, one is reminded of the scholarly perspective that renders certain portions of the Bible as non-literal, so therefore, one must be dutifully careful to see the statements, quotes and illustrative examples in the proper context. Some scholars state (Irons, p. 1 of 4) that "the issue of literal interpretation of portions of scripture over the possible use of a figurative one, as in a metaphor or illustrative parable, or other form of poetic effort to convey a larger concept or meaning is illustrated in this article to attest that the first chapter of Genesis can and must be seen as non-literal. Moses is suggested to have a larger purpose in the way of the days of Creation are presented. This is an example of how issues of interpretation beyond simple word of phrase meanings can lead to separation of groups of Christian believers." So, the immediate question is asked: "Do we accept what Jesus has to say as a direct and wholly intentional command for keeping the truth of the Gospel as he stated it to be?" If we are going to submit to the contentions of some scholars that certain aspects of the New Testament, therefore, the whole teaching on the Good News of the Kingdom of God, are not to be taken directly, but only as a story with lots of implications to be taken any way one wishes. In "Evangelical Ethics," the author tells of a UCLA professor who takes issue with the people of orthodox Christianity who are arrogant, in her words, saying: "Our present science and our present technology are so tinctured with orthodox Christian arrogance toward nature ... Is it really the case that the Bible teaches that nature exists only to serve man?" (Davis, p. 243).

In contradiction to these observations and statements of criticism for being committed to the whole truth of Jesus' teachings, we are not only reminded but also admonished with great and serious concern, by the writers of "This We Believe," that "The Gospel is the only Gospel: There is no other; and to change its substance is to pervert and indeed destroy it ... all Christians are called to unity in love and unity in truth. As evangelicals who derive our very name from the Gospel, we celebrate this great good news of God's saving work in Jesus Christ as the true bond of Christian unity, whether among organized churches and denominations or in the many trans-denominational cooperative enterprises of Christians together." (Akers, p. 240)

Living in this world today, it is not likely to run into someone who has not heard of Christianity. Yet, even within the mainline denominations, claiming historical precedence over so many groups, with so many more years (in some cases centuries), and multiple opportunities to be the true reflection of Jesus' to the world, have only persisted in perpetuating a subtle and often effective merchandizing façade of unity. Note the following: "Christian unity is the theme of the ecumenical movement. The modern ecumenical movement began in the wake of World War II as Christians came together from all sides of a war-torn world to affirm a common commitment. This, after centuries of fission and separation. This, after years of the horror of war. The old scars of Europe, the legacies of colonialism, and the denominational extravaganza of the United States have not made this work ... they are not just issues of Christian unity, but of human unity, and human relationship in a world fractured by religious division." (Eck, p. 1 of 4)

Today the church in the United States, and for that matter around the world, finds too many who are interested in Jesus, but have not been allured to his Body, the church. Elmer Towns alerts us to this issue in his book, "The Organic Church." He tells us, ' ... the world is interested in Jesus, it is His Wife (the church is the Bride of Christ) that they do not want to spend time with ... something is wrong with the way we are doing church here.' "His assessment is that too many established, facility-based churches have 'lost the plot' along the way. 'Attendance on Sundays does not transform lives; Jesus with their hearts is what changes people.' "Cole is not alone. In 'Revolution,' evangelical researcher George Barna claims that in the year 2000, most of the nation's organized religious activity took place at or through local churches. Today, according to Barna, the action is increasingly shifting to forms of religious commitment that lack any connection to the local church … these are attending a house church in the local community." (Towns, p. 26-27) In his classic book, "Classic Christianity," Bob George tells us, "After many years spent talking with people of all denominations from every part of the country, I picture the average Christian's understanding to be much as mine was: like a person with a big box of jigsaw puzzle pieces, each piece representing a Bible verse, a sermon illustration, or a doctrine they have been taught. If you have been a Christian very long at all, you have probably accumulated quite a collection! Especially in twentieth-century America, which I believe has received more Christian education than any group in the last 2000 years. All those puzzle pieces … but we don't know how to put them together!" (George, p. 69)

## The Teachings of the Disciples (Apostles)

Jesus teaches each of us to put the Kingdom of God first and His righteousness. He tells us this in the context of the Gospel of Matthew which was written by one of the Apostles who had been a tax collector. Across the many scholars and authors of texts on the book, it is mentioned that Matthew would have been the most Jewish of them all. Unlike, Mark who was half Greek, the efforts of Matthew give credence to Jesus as the real Messiah. (Howard, p. 1602)

The keys to seeking first the kingdom of God, are immeshed in the righteousness of God. (Matthew 6: 33) When one determines the need to become a child of God as a born-again Christian, a believer in Jesus and the Gospel message, then the priorities of life make a complete change … from living for our own goals and purposes to living in a cooperative, unified way with the God of

Creation through accepting the sacrifice of Jesus to pay for our sins (Book of Romans 6: 33, and Romans 10: 9-10, and John 3: 16 and 17), and give us eternal life as a free gift. Understanding the righteousness of Jesus becomes the key to being able to seek the kingdom of God first. We are taught throughout the gospels that Jesus was thoroughly involved in the relationship with His Father God. He made it clear that being in complete connection, agreement, and obedience to Him was the absolute bottom line. A perfect example of this is in the Book of John, chapter 14, where he goes into great detail about how inter-related they are ... he speaks only the words His Father gives him, he is in total agreement and is eventually going back to the realm in which the Father exists, as Jesus had been before coming to this earth. Although the disciples were slow to understand just how Jesus was going away and would be coming back with everything built and constructed (houses as an example) for the benefit of all his disciples and believers, He persisted in elaborating on the importance of being in total commitment to God's plan and life.

As Paul the Apostle became an apostle of Jesus too, he began to write letters of clarification and admonition for church groups in many cities of significance in the development of the church in Asia Minor (the basic area of Turkey today) and Greece and Macedonia. As is pointed out in the "Believer's Bible Commentary," by William MacDonald, "Our exalted standing in Christ calls for corresponding godly conduct ... as pointed out previously, these closing chapters of the letter to the Ephesians, 4-6, teach that 'we must cultivate unity in the church, purity in our personal lives, harmony in our homes, and stability in our combat with the powers of evil ... to keep the unity of the Spirit means to live at peace with one another. They should give diligence to keep the unity of the Spirit. The Holy Spirit has made all true believers one in Christ; the Body is indwelt by the one Spirit. ... denominations, sects, and parties hinder the outworking of this truth. All such man-made divisions will be swept away when the Savior returns." (MacDonald, p. 1932-1933).

This is not just a passing admonition that MacDonald discusses as presented by Paul in this key letter of the New Testament, as he addresses issue of cooperation and encouragement to grow in understanding what it means to live in cooperation not just with those within the local church homes, but to be obedient in every way that yields to God's way of love and faith. Jesus, as the High Priest, is presented as one who has followed all the plan of God, through His death and resurrection and promise to return to our planet to resurrect all those who are in relationship with God through Him. In chapter 3 of Hebrews, the author not only describes Jesus' status as the perfect sacrifice and ultimate High Priest interceding with God, His Father, for the perfection of God's overall purpose and plan for mankind, but describes Him as the one who ultimately fulfilled all the prophecies of Moses and the rest of the prophets. Seeking first the Kingdom of God and His righteousness, is the key to gaining full cooperation with those who are also called into the Body of Christ. In "How to Read the Bible for All It's Worth," the author tells us: "Note that the narrative and prayer are now followed by imperative words of exhortation. This is how Paul addresses his third major concern—that the Ephesian believers maintain 'the unity of the Spirit' noted in Ephesians 2: 11-22. Thus the exhortation to 'be filled with the Spirit' (Eph. 5:18) for worship also serves as a hinge between relationships in general and with households in particular, where worship would take place." (Fee, p. 351) Being a true believer in Jesus, the Christ and Son of God, calls for the believer to live in unity with the Spirit of God. Jesus left the disciples with the command to wait for the coming of the comforter, the Spirit of God, to be the power to live the life that enables us to seek the kingdom of God first and do so by the righteousness of God (John 20: 30-31, and I John 2: 20-23).

## The Teachings to the General Disciple Crowd

In the text, "Commentary on the Whole Bible," the author and editor takes the more negative perspective as he describes the content of Jesus' prayer in John 17 by taking issue with the observation of his review of the current situation in the church across the United States in particular as being more of a hope for what will be when Christ actually comes to Earth again. He states the following: "The 'true' body of Christ (all believers of every age) is already 'one,' as joined to the one Head. But its unity is as yet not visible, even as the Head is not visible, but shall appear when He shall appear.' (John 17: 21-23, Col. 3:4) (Jamieson, p. 1289). As Jesus began His ministry, he was deeply concerned about living a life of whole and total obedience to the plan of the Father. He spoke to the many crowds, that became a constant occurrence, as he made his way around the Judea of his ministry time. He is quoted as follows in Mark 10: 43-45, "whoever wants to become great among you must be your servant, and whoever wants to be first must be a slave of all' … if you long for greatness and a lead position, then Jesus has advice … it is working your way to the bottom to support everyone else … sadly the church had not always listened to Him. I've seen too many instances in the local church and in national bodies of believers where selfish ambition, cloaked in 'spirituality,' flatly ignores Jesus' teaching … they always put their own interests ahead of the unity of the Body of Christ." (Wood, p. 30).

In other words, again, the key to gaining the unity that the church wants that reflects the teaching of Jesus, is to take a completely different view about the behaviors, words, and actions a person must take. This world and its culture advocates taking advantage of everything and everyone to one's own benefit, regardless of the immediate or long-term impact on neighbors, friends, colleagues at work, and family. The fact of their being an over 50 percent divorce rate in the United States has been a noteworthy description of the status of family and its impact on children and general treatment of other citizens, as the determination of those who make the commitment of marriage fail to keep their word, 'for better or worse.' Unity in God's church is a goal that must be seen as it was by those Jesus addressed when presenting the message of the Kingdom of God to the people of Judea. They were immeshed in the teachings of the local synagogue, presented by rabbis, as they were admonished by the word of the High Priest and his assistants. By the time of Jesus, the Roman Empire had a total choke-hold on the local religious leaders, who perpetuated the teachings of the Old Covenant. So, as Jesus taught his basic message of the Kingdom of God, he was being reviewed, spied upon and criticized by the Jews' leadership. They saw him as a threat to their authority to work with the local Roman governor and continue to oversee and control the religious practice of the local Jews. They were committed to gaining eventual control over Judea out from under the Roman Empire, but wanted to do it under their own plan and terms. Barabbas had been a part of an insurrection against the local Roman government, and was imprisoned, to be crucified. So, it was quite a concern to the Jewish leadership, especially the high priest, that they did not need another try at a rebellion against the Romans. Jesus was effectively impacting the general populace as his healings of so many and the simple message of salvation through belief in Him was such a special and fresh presentation of the words of God. As part of Jesus' plan to bring salvation to the people of Israel (Judea) was a continual willingness to serve the needs of people who were going through a lot of personal economic issues. There were literally multiple thousands who followed the "prophet," as that was as far as they had collectively gone in recognizing Jesus as he taught them throughout the area of Judea and the surrounding areas. We know that the people were unified in their desperate need for help. However, that only went so far. Note the way Jesus was treated by those with whom he had spent his first 30 years growing up in Nazareth. In his last visit to his home town, he first goes to the synagogue to teach and ends up being denied by them, even having his family think at one point that he had lost it. (Matthew 13: 54). His self declaration was just too much for the leaders of the Jews.

## The Teachings to the Jewish Leadership

There are quite a few instances in the Gospels when a leader of the Jews confronted Jesus with a situation (which inherently required a "correct to the Law or OT" answer) to create a public declaration of Jesus' awareness of the teachings of the Pharisees and the Sadducees. Their teachings had extended the teachings of Moses, over the centuries from the time of Moses to the time of Jesus (approximately 1400 years) the Old Testament priests, prophets and other leaders, such as rabbis. Therefore since they were convinced that Jesus knew very little about the increased more technical interpretations and demands on the true Jew, it was their logical plan and intent to show Jesus to be ignorant. They saw him as just another source of disunity for their efforts to maintain their control under the permission of the Roman rulers. One of the best examples of these confrontations is the incident of Jesus being confronted with the need to pay taxes … this was an extremely powerful situation/confrontation. The Jewish leader who put this before Jesus was most certain Jesus would fail to see the implications, and certainly fail to respond to the simple question … "Teacher, we know that You speak and teach correctly, and You are not partial to any, but teach the way of God in truth. Is it lawful for us to pay taxes to Caesar, or not? (Luke 20: 21). Gary Furlong in the text "The Conflict Resolution Toolbox" gives us insight on this situation being thrown at Jesus.

He states, "How attributions form ... motives and intentions cannot be seen, they can only be inferred from our interpretation of the other party's behavior. Attributions, therefore, are fundamentally perceptions, not reality. Perceptions are influenced mostly by two factors: information and preconceptions ... still, attributions can be changed. As practitioners, we can help to influence parties' attributions by working with or challenging the two elements that form attributions, namely, information and preconceptions." (Furlong, p. 137). So, according to the author just quoted both the leader of the Jews asking the question and Jesus are confronted with the two aspects of needing to convince and declare with some realization that the opposite party is in need of having preconceptions clarified, updated, or insightfully broken down into their parts, and that the information each has must be examined for legitimacy, accuracy and practical application, knowing that time can often make information no longer useful. Of course, we know that Jesus was at a remarkably incomparable advantage as the Son of the most high God and Creator. The leader of the Jews who was representing the high priest and his concern for their status with the local Roman governing authorities (a certainly well-informed leader of the Jewish religion and its need to maintain positive political unity with the government overseeing the Palestinian province of the time), was quite certain that asking a set of particularly carefully selected questions would make them look good before any of the Roman representatives constantly surveying the situation of potential rebellion and conflict. It was the intention of this leader of the Jews to make Jesus look bad. (see Luke 20: 19-20). Once the question was asked, Jesus took a moment and simple asked to see a coin (a denarius). Then once given the coin he simply asked him. "Whose likeness and description does it have?" They all chimed in to state the name of the current Caesar ... to which Jesus replies with the most unexpected declarative statement, "Then render to

Caesar the things that are Caesar's and to God the things that are God's." They were truly amazed and unable to retort with some elaborate and intelligent and Old Covenant and Jewish leader-trained correcting comment. They were silent. They had been shut up.

But, we know that God is love (I John 4: 7-8), so there is no attempt on Jesus' part to denigrate these leaders of the Jews. His purpose was in the this instance, as it was in all such efforts to declare the ultimate truth of God's word, to proclaim God's desire to maintain peace and purpose in all situations of potential disagreement. Jesus was exemplifying before the crowd of followers and his disciples, and these leaders of the Old Testament form of God's way of life, that God is only ultimately concerned with bringing about a world of peace and hope and unity. The unity would begin in the church, yet to be established, as His own Body ... the Body of Christ, and would ultimately reign in this world at His return and finally forever in the Eternity of God's great life for all who would live His way ... the way of peace, joy, faith, and love.

There are of course other examples of Jesus presenting Himself and His kingdom to the leaders of the Jews. One other that exemplifies His authenticity and genuineness is what He had to say to another Jewish leader, a man of the Pharisees, named Nicodemus. This leader came to Jesus in the evening hours ... clearly at a time to avoid his being seen by his fellow Jewish leadership, as he more than likely still had his concerns as to the authenticity of Jesus' ministry and just exactly where Jesus might fit into the ongoing efforts of the Jews to find a place of freedom from the constant oppressive dominance of the Roman rule. He seems to be one who was willing to give Jesus a chance to further legitimize who he really was. At this point let us review one of the keys to true leadership and promoting unity in all circumstances. The writer of the "Leadership Challenge," (Kouzes, p. 10) tells us the following: "To enlist people in a vision, a leader must 'know your followers and speak their language,' according to the organizational development manager at McKesson [editor: a public company]. People must believe that you understand their needs and have their interests at heart. Only through an intimate knowledge of their dreams, their hopes, their aspirations, their visions, their values is the leader able to enlist their support." So, now we see that the very Creator of the Universe, who has become a regular human man, and has begun to present a message that is stirring the proverbial pot in the land of Judea, and especially at the capital … Jerusalem, where the Temple stands, as the very core of all the Old Testament believers stand for and believe as the evidence of God still at work in the world at that time … listens to a leader of that hierarchy who seems to come with good intent. He asks Jesus an opening question in John, chapter three, that initiates the conversation he hopes will bring further clarification to him, personally, so he can gain a greater appreciation for who Jesus really is. He, after the usual acknowledging words of recognition and complements, is answered by Jesus with, "Truly, truly, I say to you, unless one is born again he cannot see the Kingdom of God." Nicodemus actually never gets to ask a question, only introduces himself and declares what he thinks of Jesus. It is Jesus who gets down to brass tacks, and cuts to the chase on what Nicodemus was actually after. Now, Nicodemus is befuddled, taken aback at what Jesus declares so clearly, and asks, "How can a man be born when he is old? He cannot enter the second time into his mother's womb and be born, can he?" His reaction and question is simple and straightforward. He is not only caught off guard, but he is trying in the immediacy of the moment to gain some kind of understanding of what Jesus could possibly mean. Jesus explains that he is speaking of a spiritual birth, that takes place as the Spirit of God comes into a person who believes in Jesus and his message. Jesus takes issue with the fact that so many come to him for clarity on the content of his message, and fail to see it for the fact that it is different than the one that Moses brought ... it is not a message of declaring all the things one must do to be good enough to enter in a relationship with God. It is simply accepting what Jesus is saying and believing that He is the Christ as promised throughout the prophets. Nicodemus does not have anything to say after asking, "How can these things be?" Jesus declares that there is a new beginning for all who wish to follow God from now on. Paul the Apostle declares in the letter to the Ephesians, chapter four, that one must walk worthy of the calling with which you have been called, with all humility and gentleness, with patience, show tolerance for one another in love." (Paul, NASV, p. 908-909). Here Jesus was probably in a time of preparation for sleep for the night. Yet his example before Nicodemus was to ask him in and listen to his obvious interest in further information and clarity about the ministry of Jesus, and just exactly who Jesus was. So we see Jesus acting in the very manner, as his primary example before all his disciples and those thousands who followed him, that Paul continued to admonish all Jesus' followers in all his letters of apostolic urgency. Jesus saw well in advance, the completion of his own life on the Roman cross as the ultimate sacrifice for the sins of the world, so each person who believed would be motivated to respond to all they would come in contact with, as loving and patient disciples. No action and response of Jesus was to be seen only in that context of the event that occurred. What Jesus did and said had eternal value ... and Jesus carefully and wisely gave his response and teaching to Nicodemus with the future of the Church in mind. So, recently, it is the efforts of the Billy Graham Association in the latter years of Dr. Graham's ministry to again reach out to the United States with an urgent appeal to awaken to the Gospel (Graham, p. 40). His son, Franklin wrote, "In the past five decades, our nation seems to have done everything it can to marginalize the role of faith and religion in our society. The rise of pluralism and tolerance has sought to dilute the influence of Christianity." Jesus knew of this situation in our nation today, even as he was responding to Nicodemus. He saw a deeply rooted defensiveness that would cloud and create a wide-ranging spread of disbelief in the basic message of the Gospel. How can a person gain a relationship with the Creator God without working so very hard at becoming worthy of that relationship by one's own works, decisions, goodness and legacy? So, even though there was the immediate need to answer the questions of Nicodemus, Jesus was constantly aware of the implications and example his words and actions would have for the long-term in the development of the Body of Christ … His Own Body.

# CHAPTER SIX

# Paul the Apostle and Other Writers' Teaching

As we look at some specific representations of Paul the Apostle's teachings and the rest of the New Testament authors more in depth, it is important to realize they wrote based on a set of clear and unarguable facts. They wrote based on their personal relationship with Jesus Christ. Whether they new Him personally as he involved them in his ministry throughout the three and a half years of presenting the Gospel message, or learned of Him through others who in fact were one of those who actually spent time with Jesus, they were committed to continuing what Jesus so wonderfully and consistently taught.

## Paul the Apostle's Teaching

This apostle came after the original twelve plus the one who took Judas Iscariot's place. He was put through a time of personally espousing his commitment to eliminating these people of the "Way." It was on one of these many missions, authorized by the High Priest of Jerusalem, that Jesus caught his attention, and confronted him directly with his massive ignorance and blindness to the truth that Jesus taught. The same truth Jesus presented to Nicodemus the night he made an effort to understand just exactly who Jesus was. Paul was a servant to the leaders of the Jewish religion, based on interpretations of the Old Testament that had been developed into a document called the Talmud. Their understanding, and Paul's, was based on what would today be called a "pre-determined view." A New York Times author and Christian believer upon being interviewed by a reporter for the magazine, "Christianity Today," declared that this was his own personal finding based on his work as a reporter. (Gladner, p. 53). Paul was obsessed with the teachings he had from the great Judean teacher, Gamaliel. He was a complete devotee to keeping the religion of the Jewish people alive and established, and eventually freed from the impact of the oppressive Roman empire. He wanted a unified religious status. He wanted to be a significant part of the effort to protect his religion.

After Paul was confronted with the truth of the "Way," and was healed to see again the real truth of Jesus (a tremendous figurative example of one being blind to the truth and being healed to see the new covenant, with salvation being purchased and made freely available to all who would believe in the work, life, death and resurrection of Jesus), he became as much a fervent follower of Jesus as anyone in the history of Christianity. He was so committed that his writings, the letters he wrote and the biography by Luke of the work the Paul conducted (the major portion of the book of Acts of the Apostles) focused heavily on the need for unity. Note the words Paul wrote in the first letter to the Corinthian church: "Now I exhort you, brethren, by the name of our Lord Jesus Christ, that you all agree and that there be no divisions among you, but that you be made complete in the same mind and in the same judgment" (I Corinthians 1: 10). Paul goes on throughout this first letter to the brethren in Corinth to exhort and admonish them to conduct themselves in a way of living that reflected patience and kindness. His incredible definition of what the love of God is all about, in chapter 13, gives completed understanding that God's way is a way of service, humility and working in every way to be together in attitude, motivation, actions and decisions. He concludes by stating that of the three keys to living the Christian life, faith, hope and love, love is the foundation upon which they will find success in making their life count for the promotion and building of the Gospel and maturing of the church. In the second book to the brethren in Corinth, Paul concludes his admonishments by declaring his firm intent to look for evidence of their improved commitment to the truth. As is stated in "The Complete Guide to the Bible," regarding another letter he wrote to new Christian believers in the city of Ephesus, "Paul calls for unity in the churches, but not unity at all costs (Eph. 4) … for he warns as documented by Luke in Acts 20:30, 'some men from your own group will rise up and distort the truth in order to draw a following … he goes on in Ephesians 4 to confront these people, but in peace, for there is one Lord, faith, baptism, God and Father." In the letter Paul writes to the Galatians he cuts to the chase right off the bat, when he states, "I am amazed that you are so quickly deserting Him who called you by the grace of Christ, for a different gospel; which is really not another; only there are some who are disturbing you and want to distort the gospel of Christ" (Galatians 1: 6-7). Here Paul is not only disturbed by the fact that these believers are so easily influenced by others coming into their house church and causing them to lose faith and trust in the truth that Paul had taught so diligently and extensively, but that they are not striving to find some way to verify and re-establish what they were first taught … just giving in to the next bunch of "evangelists" that come along. His long-term concern is the need for them, as well as all groups of believers, to find ways to mature in the faith.

In the letter that Paul wrote to the Romans, he makes the

unifying, generic and all-encompassing statement regarding the power of the righteousness of Christ (Romans 10:4), declaring, "For there is no distinction between Jew and Greek (this being the particular term of the time in which Koine Greek meant those who were not Jews ... the entirety of the rest of humanity, and often also used was "heathen"); for the same Lord is Lord of all, abounding in riches for all who call on Him; for 'Whosoever will call on the name of Lord will be saved'" (Romans 10: 12-13) As Paul continued his ministry he was constantly called upon to speak in the local synagogue as he visited the cities and areas God inspired him to attend. More than often, once he got past his declaration of who he was as committed believer in the teachings of the prophets and Moses, he would begin his declaration of the work of Jesus the Christ. It was at this point the people in the synagogue would either listen further and have other questions, or would immediately take issue with his presentation, asking him to leave or threatening his life. Maintaining the unity of the Jews was certainly a concern for Paul, as his introductory words most often attempted to say to the synagogue group that he was one of them ... he just now had a special additional message from God about His Son who was killed by the Jews of Jerusalem. Note the example of Paul's entry into Jerusalem after a few days of visiting the temple. The Jews from Asia, cried out, "Men of Israel, come to our aid! This is the man who preaches to all men everywhere against our people, and the Law and this place; and besides he has even brought Greeks into the temple and had defiled this holy place" (Acts 21: 27-28). Despite his continual efforts to promote a preaching/presentation of the gospel message that was rooted in the Old Testament or the Law, Paul was in the long-run unable to gain the acceptance by the Jews holistically. They fought him to the very end on the topic of unity, in that they only saw his efforts as an effort on his part to create disunity among the Jews as believers as declared by Moses and the prophets. Paul never let up on being factual and accurate to the Word (Jesus Christ) of God. In the magazine, "Israel My Glory," the author of "Why We Believe," wrote: " ...this should not come as a surprise, as God's Word tells us the same thing: 'The Spirit Himself bears witness with our spirit that we are the children of God (Romans 8: 16). Why do you believe? Because God's truth is factual, intellectually coherent, and consistent with real life. And when we trust in His Son, God imprints it indelibly on our hearts" (Parshall, p. 13) Paul was intent on being attendant to the truth of God's Word. His diligence and faithfulness to God's Word caused him to see the absolutely essential truth that being at one with God in all things, also required that each member of the Body of Christ be in unity by the Spirit of God. This unity was a new variation for the original Christian believers (believers of the "Way"), as they were 100% Jews. Now they had to embrace all others, which required a totally new sense of what being in unity meant. The Bible teaches that God's Word will not return void. What God has planned, in this case for all mankind, is going to be perfectly worked out ... no obstacle will thwart the work of the Creator of the Universe. Satan and his demons and the influential culture of this world will not in anyway succeed. Death is defeated, in Christ's victory over it. Each Christian has been given eternal life as a free gift. The final unification of all creation is merely a matter of time until the return of Jesus Christ.

## Teachings from Other New Testament Writers of Books and Letters

At this point it is critical to present a remarkable aspect to the consistency of the writings of the New Testament books and letters. The inerrancy of Scripture is a critical point across the entire Bible. When one reviews the content of the 27 canonical texts, it is clear that the basic message of the Gospel of Jesus Christ is dutifully attended to by all eight authors of the New Testament books/letters with no contradictions. In the text, "Introduction to Biblical Interpretation," the author states, "(re: content of the entire Bible) This final element is more controversial and more difficult to control. As we presupposed, the Bible possesses a unity in its parts in spite of its diversity of human authors. Scripture's divine inspiration gives continuity of thought to books written over a 1500 year period ... Because of this unity, the entire Bible provides a literacy context for all passages in it. But here comes the controversy and the difficulty. How do we allow individual authors their unique perspective—the Bible's diversity—and yet affirm the Bible's unity?" (Klein, p. 168) Obviously, human experts on language, biblical interpretation both as one language to the other and the historical significance of biblical content in the light of word and phrase meanings, cannot be the final source of determining the validity of the content of the books/letters and overall presentation of the New Testament in total. It is self-proclaimed in each book/letter that Jesus Christ and his life, death and resurrection totality message is the foundation of all truth, purpose, life protocol and benefits. When Peter, the chief apostle, to whom Jesus said, "upon this rock I will build my church," (Matthew 16:18), he was singled out as a significant leader of the Church to be after the Day of Pentecost. He became the one would introduce the entire Jesus message to the Jewish and Hellenistic Jewish world. He wrote two books/letters to the church in general, about the necessity of keeping to the foundational message of the teachings of Jesus. In chapter two of I Peter, he advocates a spirit and behavior of unity by admonishing all Christians, whether slave or leader to by in a state of humility to those with whom they must live and work.

Even today, there are church congregations that advocate going back to the origin of Christian belief and not allow historical changes, and other developing over time traditions change the basic beliefs from the Bible only. "By and large, most sectors of evangelical Protestantism have "restoration movement" mentality. We regularly look back to the church and Christian experience in the first century either as the norm to be restored or the ideal to be approximated." (Fee, p. 88)

Referring back to the Apostle Paul, more than anything, due to his major contribution to the entirety of the New Testament texts, we find a commendation and distinctive observation from one of the current scholars on the issue of leadership, as a part of the overall effort Paul addresses in motivating those who take on those roles in the local congregation. Paul regularly reminds the leaders to remain in the Spirit of Christ, one of servant humility. Note the comment in the text entitled, "Theology of the New Testament," by one of our current scholars: "There is no clearly defined office of leadership in the Pauline congregations. The reality of the Body of Christ was the overarching concept, and the unity and unanimity of the church that had within it the functions of community leadership without needing to make claims of hierarchical office, for the fundamental operative principle was: church leadership is a charisma, a gift of the Holy Spirit. No one has the right to set this or that gift absolutely above the others in which the reality of the Spirit's presence in the congregation was experienced." (Strecker, p. 191)

In the text, "A Topical Dictionary of Bible Texts," the author/editor shows a listing of at least 12 references describing Church Unity directly: "John 10:16, John 17:11, Romans 12:4, I Corinthians 10:17 12: 5, Galatians 3:26, Ephesians 1:10, 2:15, 3:6, 4:4, 4:16, Colossians 3:11." This listing included only direct references, as there are other ones, such as those in Acts, obviously imply the necessity and whole-hearted intention towards unity within the church and among the brethren.

**James in another profoundly important author of a New Testament book.** His relationship with Jesus and his leadership with the Jerusalem church was an incredible place of insight and solid understanding of the purpose of God's Church, the Body of Christ Jesus. It was his influence that authorized the formal acceptance of the gospel to the Gentiles (Heathen, Non-Jews). That was an awesome decision and obviously has had impact and foundational beginning to the Church worldwide today.

Paul obviously took the decision further and gave it a very detailed and careful definition to what constitutes a completely different "religion" than what was in place at the time of the crucifixion of Jesus under the High Priest and his cohorts. What had been a religion, was now a relationship with the Creator for each and every one who accepted the work and teaching of Jesus as Lord and Savior. A brand new belief system in the God of the Universe was in place. In the text, "Exploring Theology," the author states: "The Christians united not only as a church, but as a family. Many Jewish converts were ostracized by their families and friends; so the Christians helped and encouraged one another. Their mutual faith in the Messiah bound them together as a group. And the Holy Spirit worked mightily as a result of their unity." He goes on to state, "They recognized their vital need for fellowship and remained steadfast in it. If the members had stopped to criticize, no doubt they would have found faults in each other. Instead, they were quick to see their own failures, but slow to criticize others." (Benson, p. 173)

In the Holman Christian Standard Bible commentary notes, the editor of this text states, "Believers have the responsibility to keep unity in the Body of Christ. The seven 'ones' enumerated in these verses [Ephesians 4: 1-6] constitute the foundation on which the Trinitarian God creates a oneness of the church. Paul's plan can be seen from the vantage point of the work of one Spirit, creating one body, the one Lord Jesus Christ creating one hope, faith, and baptism, and the one God the Father bringing about one people of God … One God and Father of all reminds believers that God's oneness defines the church's oneness." (Howard, p. 2003). In another recent online article, "Biblical Principles of the Unity of the Church," the author states: "The church is the covenant people of God in all ages and among all nations … in the New Testament this teaching of the unity of the people of God is sustained … the unity of the church is attained unto by growing in spiritual maturity (referencing Eph. 4 again). As we take account of the diversity that exists between denominations arising from differences of ethnic identity, cultural background, and historical circumstance the conclusive evidence derived from scripture is required to support the position that the obliteration of denominational separateness is an obligation resting upon these church of Christ … though the diversity which manifests itself in differentiating historical development might appear to make ecclesiastical union inadvisable or even perilous in certain cases, yet the biblical evidence in support of union is so plain that any argument to the contrary, however plausible, must be false." (No author listed, www.opc.org/relations/unity, p. 1-9). James reaches out to the 12 tribes of Israel in his opening introductory sentences, recognizing that the newly developing Christian church was spreading across what was to become Europe and the Middle East/Turkey, basically all around the Mediterranean Sea, and the Roman Empire as it spread as well. He sees that there will be Contentions and problems associated with economic status, ethnicities and other cultural and language differences. He knows the work of Paul, as he authorized it … so he takes the trouble to address those matters of potential conflict. He reminds the readers of the need for acts of kindness and patience, suggesting that a regular request for wisdom from God does so much to promote unifying attitudes and environments in the church groups meeting in believers' homes throughout the empire. He takes issue with those who want to continue to require the standard Jewish protocols and points out the value of watching what one says, especially as to the attitudes behind those pronouncements. James could see far beyond his shortened life, to the value of yielding to God each day and remaining humble before the other believers, but also before the jurisdictions of the empire. He asks them to remember to stay focused on what you do have, being joyful in God's provision, but never hesitating to go before God to ask for the necessities, from daily needs to healing to protections. An author of the text, "Primal," reminds us even today of the same admonitions of James, when he states: "None of Us can imagine what God is capable of. Which means none of us can imagine what we're Capable of if we give God control of our lives. His power sets off a chain reaction. And with His energy at work within us, there is nothing we can't do ... but many of us never 'flip the switch.' We never receive the power He promised. And without His power, we become nothing more than theological Christians ... with His power at work within us, we cannot accomplish His purposes." (Batterson, p. 153).

# CHAPTER SEVEN

# Gleaning the Deficits that
# Undermine Unity

A review of the 1600 plus denominational groups who claim to adhere to the Christian faith as proclaimed in the New Testament of the Bible, per the recent Pew research of Christian groups in the United States alone, shows a distinct and outspoken intent to remain as they are. There are efforts, as mention earlier, to promote a grouping, association and adherence to a larger common unity, as seen in the National Association of Evangelicals and the National Council of Churches. So, at least from the current practice of any organized effort, whether sports' teams, school systems, educational institutions, clubs for any number of interests, and even such groups as charities and efforts to support military wounded, an advertizing and merchandizing legacy is promoted to convey a cooperativeness to the general public. As an example, there is a national association, regionally organized, to certify the legitimacy of university and college degrees as meeting specific standards, like the "Western Association of Schools and Colleges." Before any enrolling student is actually committed to a college, they want to be assured that the national association of certifying the standards of excellence in collegiate training has certified the college or university they plan to attend. Most anyone wants to get the best for their dollar. In the area of Christian groups/denominations/associations there is a more intense and intentional effort to advertize the value and benefit of being a part of that particular grouping than ever before. On one side of it, there is the proclaimed and often announced intention to "proclaim the Good News ... the Gospel of Jesus Christ," yet juxtaposed with that clear and constant message is a well-planned and intentional message of "come to our group because ..." listing all the great reasons why one should attend our church, join our association, contribute to our charitable group, or use our Christian materials or devices for presenting the Christian message.

It is not uncommon for a person who is considered an expert on a particular topic to advise the person needing guidance to "step back and gain a much wider perspective or vision of the entire context in which a concern, problem or issue needs to be seen." Often it involves financial review in a larger perspective, as well as, such matters of maintenance of the facilities associated with the Christian group, so as to continue the goals, and visions of the groups administrators. When the leadership and members of a particular group are focused on the goals and vision, it is their intent to maintain and continually make reviews to promote adjustments to the overall effort to enable growth and vitality to continue, often at an ever increasing rate.

## Denominational Rise: Main Reasons for Separation

Aubrey Malphurs, in his book, "Developing a Vision for Ministry in the 21st Century," gives us a clear statement about the need for unity in a group of any Christian community. He states, "An institutional vision is one of the critical components of unity in ministry. The vision affects at least two areas of organizational unity ... the first area of unity is in the recruitment of ministry personnel. The can decide in advance if their personal vision closely matches the organization's direction ... the second area is in the retention of ministry personnel ... New Testament ministry is team ministry (Acts 11: 22-30, etc.), who make significant but different contributions from their gifts and varied personalities ... vision is the leaders key to holding the team together." (Malphurs, p. 20) When Jesus spoke to the issue of vision in his prayers of John 17, he was focused on unity being the essential aspect of relationship ... He with the Father God, and the Father God with Him. In another text written by an author already referred to in a previous portion of this paper, he tells us, "Paul the Apostle argues first that the many of them (Jew, Gentile, slave, free) are one body because of their common lavish experience of Spirit (I Cor. 12) ... likewise, in Philippi, where some bickering and posturing were going on that could lead to disunity, Paul urges his readers, especially in light of their struggle against pagan opponents, to 'stand firm in one Spirit' (Phil. 1: 27) ... unity in the body means that believers 'walk by the Spirit' so as not to eat and devour one another (Gal. 3) ... it also requires heterogeneous people to submit their diversity to the unifying work of the Spirit ... such churches cannot maintain the unity of the Spirit that Paul taught in Ephesians 2 and 4 and I Corinthians 12." (Fee, p. 71) Running any organization, whether the Ford Motor Company, the nation of Russia, or the local Christian denominational congregation, requires among many things, the efforts of the leadership to stay close to the guiding laws, principles, protocols and procedures, whether for the long-haul or the day-to-day duties. Mr. Ronald Reagan had some direct commentary about the problems of the United States government: "Reagan's alternative vision of federalism can be summarized in three phases: 'separation of powers,' 'devolution of responsibilities to governments that are closer to the people,' and 'less spending by all levels of government' ... it is now argued that lines of accountability have been blurred by this overlapping of authority across the three distinct powers of the federal government." (Palmer, p. 222). As we step back and look at the current governmental difficulties our nation of America is experiencing as acknowledged by most political perspectives, one of the key issues is that the bureaucratic daily conduct has actually caused the distinctiveness of the Congress, the Presidency and the Supreme Court to blend so much in so many ways that the actual ties to the roots of the United States Constitution are no longer clearly connected. All sides claim that the Courts are presuming to make decisions that are not founded by the statements of the constitution, and the Departments of the Presidency are not dutifully following the intent of the Congress's laws that are made with a clear intent. So, we have a historically developing problem that argues that the founding document of the United States is not being following directly but much more subjectively to adjust to the more modern situations of oversight and running a much more complex government. Just as president saw a major problem developing in the implementation of the United States governance, so the Apostle Paul and other writers of the New Testament saw developing problems wholly out of step with the truth of the Gospel Message of Jesus. He addressed the need to diligently focus on the needs of one another and dwell on the effort to serve one another, instead of finding fault so easily. There were too many other 'evangelists' who were only in it to gain their own acclaim and continually focused on keeping the Jewish practices ... even Peter was caught doing that very thing (Galatians 2).

In one author's efforts to organize to promote unity in the church, he states: "Spend more time considering evidence of grace than the sins of others. Spiritual safety comes through unity ... when one isolates oneself by disrupting or denying unity, than one is most at risk. Meditate on God's many commands to love one another (i.e., Jn. 15: 12, I Jn. 4: 7, I Pet. 1: 22). Focus on the areas of agreement than on those of disagreement. Remember that God is a God of peace … making our peace with God obligates making peace with others. Preach peace to yourself, as God has forgiven you, be more tolerant of others. Dwell on the admonition in Ps. 133:1 … 'how good and pleasant it is for brothers to dwell together in unity.' Remind oneself of the cost to the church when disunity is perpetuated … Satan wins. Take the initiative to promote unity on your own, not waiting for others to start it or promote it … be an instigator with joy and love. Let God's word be the judge, so one can focus on working together rather than scrutinizing the work and motivations of others. Focus on self -judging my own actions and motivations in the light of God's word rather than of brothers. Pursue humility to promote the attitude of a servant, as Jesus Gave the example to the disciples even as he was to endure death and horrible punishments." (Editor, http://www.challies.com, p. 1 of 5). The "Peacemaker Church" has a manual that they use to govern the unity within their group. "Unity: we usually resolve disagreements over vision and goals in a constructive manner. The spirit of harmony and sincere love in our church allows us to work toward our goals effectively. Our leaders seek true unity (sincere agreement) rather than an imposed uniformity. The power of the gospel is revealed in our church by a growing unity, harmony, and stability in marriages, leadership, and membership. Peacemaking has helped people resolve conflicts that otherwise might have caused them to leave our church, people seldom leave our church because of personal conflicts." (Sande, p. 185) That is a great status of things for that particular group in Montana, but for most churches there is a constant factor of gaining and losing. "78.4 percent of U.S. citizens connect to Christian religion. Foreign born Christian adherents are two to one Catholic over Protestant. The survey finds that constant movement characterizes the American religious marketplace, as every major religious group is simultaneously gaining and loving adherents." (Editor, Pew Research, p. 1 of 3) Since leadership in every since is a huge factor in the success of any group, Christian, or simply out in the every day work world (businesses, corporations, associations and school systems, for example), it is critical that for the sake of promoting unity, whether in our out of the church that we examine the research on leaders. A rather interesting portion of a text on leadership, tells us: "(General Systems Theory) For several centuries our culture, with its Western European beginnings, has looked at the structure of experience using a mechanistic worldview. According to this view, the world is much like a machine make of component parts all working together in synchronized fashion to some purposeful end. To understand that world and one's place and purpose in it, break the larger machine into its component parts and seek to understand the individual parts and how they work together ... there are other ways, different languages, and less mechanistic ideas that we can use to help us to understand and to respond to our congregations more appropriately. Systems theory provides a helpful, more organic language and ideas that give rise to more appropriate responses, responses beyond solving problems and seeking control ... focusing on nourishing and nurturing the system, not just fixing it." (Rendle, p. 52-53).

As John Maxwell, the respected Christian writer on leadership in both the Christian church, but across all work situations, tells us, "We are not here to compete with each other, but to complete each other ... Theodore Roosevelt said, 'the best executive is one who has the sense enough to pick good men to do what he wants done, and the self-restraint enough to keep from meddling with them while they do it.'" (Maxwell, p. 73, 189).

Dealing with the entirety of leaders and the execution of oversight and promotion of the goals and visions of the local congregation, are intertwined with the practices learned in the world of business and other practical job-related environments (military, large families, associations like alumni and fraternities/ sororities, for example). So the leaders of the church are highly influenced by the leadership practices seen in their own personal development in usually public education, some in military, and having had part-time or other types of jobs growing up. One thing is for sure, and that is the incredibly significant and powerful influence of local group leadership. A. W. Tozer, in his remarkable book, "The Pursuit of God," tells us one of the critical keys to unity: "Much of our difficulty as seeking Christians stems from our own unwillingness to take God as He is, and adjust our lives accordingly. We insist upon trying to modify Him and to bring Him nearer to our own image." (Tozer, p. 101) Along with his foundational critique of the basic issues of unity in the church, we are advised by another author of one of the key problems he noticed over time as he toured a variety of congregations in the United States. He writes, "But in the beginning is grace. In the middle is grace. In the end, 'all manner of things shall be well' (Julian of Norwich) because of grace. What I'm hearing time and again, in every corner of the church I visit, is not the soaring message of grace, but a dull message of works—that I have a certain feeling, or perspire in effort before I can be assured of God's radical acceptance and my future salvation." (Galli, p. 23-24) So as we take a closer look at denominations and the various ways the Christian Church, the Body of Christ, is being developed, attended to, treated and taught, we find inherent issues of division that are founded often times on the most subtle impacting issues. The leadership of any organization is looked to for more than just information, and additional training on how to do the job. They are looked to for example … how to do what needs to be done, and how to do it with the greatest probability of reaching the goals and vision of the organization. However, keeping a balance about leading the congregation, in the case of the modern situation in Christian churches, is not an easy responsibility. From the website of the Church of Christ, comes an article on over century-long history of the local congregation in a town in Tennessee. The author tells that, "The Bible vividly portrays the nature of the church in the various descriptive titles. These show its relationship to Christ and to the world, as well as the relationship one to another ... as a body, it is united. No member is unnecessary, each cares for the other, and all joined to the Head (I Corinthians 12). (Editor, http://www.mtjuliet. org, p. 7). As the leadership considers the daily regimen of the congregational oversight, one of the things that is often left minimally attended to is the need for each and every member of the group to know his or her place of importance. Author Christian Cleveland wrote in one of her articles for Intervarsity Christian Fellowship, commented on by one of the editors of the text: "Cleveland takes a different tack and examines many of the social factors that inhibit the church's desire for unity ... not discounting the theological issues, while challenging her readers to examine biases and presuppositions that govern the way they interact with the 'other.'" (Cleveland, p. 1 of 3) If a person or persons within a group have some concerns about another one in the group they should be thoroughly advised by the leadership as to how one goes about even considering addressing those concerns or issues. In the commentary of the Ryrie Study Bible, the author gives explanation for the urgings of Paul the Apostle in chapter twelve of I Corinthians: "(I Cor. 12: 12-31) Here Paul describes the relationship of gifted believers to each other, using the analogy of the human body. The Spirit has formed a spiritual organic unity of the many dissimilar members of the Body of Christ. The constitutions both of the human body and the Body of Christ demand that all members (even those that seem unimportant) function in harmony." (Ryrie, p. 1426). Getting along has always been a matter of concern for the leadership of the church, from the very beginnings. As alluded to earlier in this paper, the Acts of the Apostles describes the fact that widows of the Hellenist group were being allegedly overlooked in services by those able to attend to their needs within the growing New Testament church. This caused the very foundational group of leaders, the Apostles established on the Day of Pentecost after Jesus went back to the Father, to stop and regroup regarding how the leaders of the church would be attending to the body of believers. This foundational decision to appoint and select deacons, or servants, was critical to giving organization to the overall services of the Body of Christ. This was a matter of physical needs not being met. This was not a spiritual matter, of not (in modern context and terms) being able to make Wednesday night bible study, because a person was in need of a ride to the church building. Or, needing counseling as to the bible teaching on how to conduct oneself in pre-marriage dating. This was a genuinely needy situation, but was apparently not in the context of the thinking of Apostles as the church was enjoying such remarkable growth, with thousands believing their message of the Gospel and coming into the faith. Of course, they were all Jews, thinking in cultural terms and localized perspectives as to what the routines were of people, and families and local thinking on what was to occur when a older lady, without her husband was to be treated and taken care of. Since those around Jerusalem were in their normal context, and were comfortable about how things were being handled, as the church joined in common house groups for being taught the truth of the Gospel by the apostles and other leading men and women, they had not given any significant, if any at all, thought to those who were from other areas, cities and locations who had come to celebrate the festivals in Jerusalem. Now they were being segregated from members of their families who had traveled with them, because they had believed this strange non-orthodoxy … non-Old Testament belief of the "Way." It was only natural for any of the Hellenistic widows if coming into the Christian faith to be left without family support, as the Rest of their family ostracized them as "unclean." Just as the Samaritan woman was shocked that Jesus even spoke to her, since their cultural ties were long severed, so these widows were probably doubly desperate, having made the commitment to Christ, realizing more each day that their lives were going through a dramatic change, especially away from the demands of orthodoxy, and now their own families were leaving them unattended and disenfranchised. The unity of the faith had not yet fully been realized, as they could not get support from the growing Body of Christ, as they were "family-less."

Ibrahim Kalin, in his internet website article, "Religion, Unity and Diversity," states the following regarding unity: "The terms unity, integration and diversity have multiple layers of meaning in the Religious context ... when understood properly, unity does not mean uniformity ... diversity does not mean disorder ... a broader understanding of these terms will help and lead us to a more critical assessment of the Enlightenment and Western modernity ... conceptually, our minds conceive things not as discrete and disconnected items, but as an interconnected unity ... it is the unity between heaven and earth that generates order, proportion, balance and harmony in the world." (Kalin, p. 1 of 7). He urges us to not be too restrictive in our respect for the need for unity. We need to respect the rights of others to gain their level of understanding and insight regarding the message of the Gospel at the degree of progression they are able to handle the teachings of Christ ... and the time and circumstances needed to practice what they have been taught and learned in their own study of the Bible. True, there are key aspects of what Jesus taught, that are absolutely core fundamentals, that cannot be modified or minimized. According to Craig Parshall in his article, entitled "A More Perfect Union: The Biblical Bottom Line," we must maintain and defend the truth at all costs ... as Jesus said, "I am the Way, the Truth and the Life, no man can come unto the Father except by Me." (John 14:6) He goes on to state: "Biblical fidelity and the belief in the authenticity and plenary inspiration of Scripture is becoming increasingly important for the church, particularly as America continues its downward slide from being irritably impatient to condemning those who take the Bible seriously. As things progress, the church will be tempted to avoid clearly teaching the Word." (Parshall, p. 13) As denominations deal with life in the current modern, continually revising culture here in the Western world, it is critical that the leaders of denominations and local congregations/groups sets a high standard of being founded on every word of God in the Bible. A recent article in the Good News magazine, a periodical of the United Church of God, ask the question, most relevant: "What Do You Believe and Why?" He asks: "How do you know if what you believe is really true? Is it possible you have been influenced to believe things that are wrong? How does it happen ... it's because their views have been formed as a result of tradition, hearsay or information not based on fact or properly researched. (Conventional beliefs regarding the Sabbath and how long Jesus was in the grave before his resurrection are listed as ideas not supported by what the New Testament actually states ... editor)." This is an example of the way in which each denomination asserts its legitimacy and why anyone reviewing their status in the context of all Christian groups should clearly select them as the group to become a part of. (LaBissoniere, p. 28-29) This particular denomination is a splinter off a previously regenerated Christian group that was labeled a cult by evangelical scholars. It did a complete revision of their beliefs to the extent they were accepted into the National Association of Evangelicals back In 1997. Their turnaround was documented in a number of published works and was certified in the publication, "Christianity Today." This would be an excellent example of the effort to by major denominations and scholars at the many theological seminaries to maintain the clearly distinguishable characteristics of each and every larger and well-known Christian body/group. In Walter Martin's classic book, "Kingdom of the Cults," he tells us a recent description of the group of modern "Christian believers," called the New Age movement. He states, "The New Age movement is not easily defined. It has no specific founder, primary leader, central headquarters, organizational structure, or definitive statement of beliefs. Nor does it meet in any one place or at any one particular time. It is not even limited to one single group. As a result the New Age movement is described in a variety of ways ... they hold many common beliefs, but often hold numerous distinctive doctrines ... even disagreeing with each other on significant issues ... they do not fit the classic definition of a cult." (Martin, p. 333).

This is not just a problem with a newer religious convocation of believers, as it has been a characteristic of church groups from the very beginning, even in the more recent beginnings of the United States. Take the historical description of a local congregation in Tennessee. The author of this short article tells us, "The third question of interest is why the split caused by the liberal element was so late in making its influence felt here. The movement started in the 1800's and the split was complete by 1906, yet it was evidently 1915 before the brethren became alarmed ... Bro. Elam's text states 'this property is to be used only for a House of Worship for a congregation of the Church of Christ. It is a condition of this conveyance (the deed) without which it would not be made, that the use of instrumental music in the worship at all times be forbidden.'" (Cathon, p. 1 of 2) The leadership of the local congregation has got to maintain the core values of the particular version of Christianity, often to the detriment of the wholistic intentions of the New Testament for unity. Too often, as in this instance, the local tradition/protocols of worship, attendance, and conduct are the primary concerns of the local leadership. It is most common to see that the initiation of a "newer version" of the Christian church groups, is provoked and over time initiated by the leadership of the local church congregation … not so much the regional or national association's leadership. For example note the instance that recently occurred in a large United States denomination.

In a recent issue of the Tennessean Newspaper, an article referred to the Southern Baptist Convention: "Not all Baptists agree with the resolution [calls for immigration reform but asks all congregations to assist undocumented aliens in need]." (Smietana, p. local news sect. 2013). This relates to the whole continuing responsibility of the individual Christian believer and the responsibility of the local pastors/teachers/leaders to use the well-researched skills for human cooperative efforts. There are literally thousands of books that have been published since the time of the industrial revolution that started in Europe and spread to the United States and eventually all around the world's major nations. In these books, the authors have almost always included recommendations for promoting inter-relationships between owners, board members chief executives and the employees that they are responsible for guiding and overseeing during the accomplishments of goals, services to consumers and succeeding as a business in an ever-growing business world. These books, often used as textbooks in college and university classes on the topic of succeeding and dealing with business responsibilities, are constantly referring to the best practices, strategies and approaches to promoting unity and a cooperative effort that ends up helping and benefitting all involved. Even as the Southern Baptist Convention meets to deliberate on the "doctrinal" beliefs, policies and public representations it wants promoted and encouraged across all local congregations in agreement with the national association, there is an effort to present, explain, accommodate and tie the basic ideas, proposals and general presentation of the association's official and formal stand on a particular subject to the founding principles of the Bible. This is not always an easy, quick to be done action. There are various understandings, often based on fairly subjective traditions, teachings, and even too often, very simplistic actual knowledge on the topic of conflict. Even though each side, in their effort to make their position clear, will go to such a clearly understandable passage of the New Testament as Ephesians, chapter four, the capacity to see it ultimately as the others are explaining is too often colored by those individuals shallow or incomplete grasp of what a passage like Ephesians chapter four actually means. Walter Harrelson, in the "New Interpreter's Study Bible," explains, "These verses (Eph. 4: 1-16) explain why the church is unified, and what behaviors make for unity ... (4: 4-6) lists the seven (perfect number) reasons for church unity." (Harrelson, p. 2094). That is just the issue for almost all points of disagreement, often on matters that are certainly secondary in priority as to the truth ... core principles of Christian belief. As an author of an article in the magazine of the United Church of God explains from their perspective: "Traditional beliefs about heaven and hell are based on an underlying teaching—that everyone has an immortal soul that must go somewhere when physical life ends. This belief isn't unique to traditional Christianity, 'All religions affirm that there is an aspect of the human person that lives on after physical life has ended ... in other words, in general, some kind of immortal essence, a spirit that lives on separately after the physical body dies. Most professing Christians call this the immortal soul.'" (Horner, p. 6) Such matters of disagreement are certainly sufficient to create division. It is simple and straightforward understandings that are in contrast to the same topic of belief in another Christian group that create the mass of divisions in the huge listing of denominations across just the United States. We are at a recent count of over 1600 incorporated and separate Christian groups. Each one stands for the beliefs they hold with great determination and affirmation of their desire to maintain and continue their separate efforts to address the obligations of living for Christ. On one side of it, it is certainly commendable, but looking at it from the overall Body of Christ perspective, it is not what was advocated by Jesus (John 17) and his apostle Paul (Ephesians 4) which we see explained again in the work of Merrill Tenney, "The New Testament Survey," as he states: "Ephesians is a specimen of his 'Bible Conference' technique. [referring to Paul and his writing technique and appeal to the church members]. Much of its material can be duplicated in his other epistles, and there is little theology or ethics in Ephesians that cannot be found in essence elsewhere. The total complex, however, in integrated into a new picture of the church as a single functioning body, created out of Jew and Gentile, equipped with standards of its own, and engaged in a spiritual conflict. It's goal is 'unity of the faith ... knowledge of the Son of God ... the increase of the stature of the fullness of Christ (Ephesians 4: 13).'" (Tenney, p. 321) It is the intent of so many to present a façade and implication of togetherness, and willingness to work together. But, obviously, with what has been presented so far, the goal of unity of the Body of Christ seems to be something to be achieved only after Christ returns at His second-coming when all will be miraculously joined in spirit bodies at the resurrection.

## Conflict with the Bible by Today's Christianity

As has been pointed out previously, the intentions of the heart, both of the individual Christian believer, and the groups of Christians in any of the many associations (church congregation, church house group, or actual corporations of Christian service or evangelization), seems to genuinely advocate unity. But the practical demonstration of that alleged desire for unity is so often undermined by the simplest of ongoing matters of organization and perpetuation of the organization.

One effort is described in an article in the Huffington Post, made available just this past July 2014. It reads as follows: "Currently, the Protestant churches recognize Roman Catholic Baptisms, but the Catholic church does not always recognize theirs. The mutual agreement on baptisms, a key sacrament in the churches, has been discussed between denominational leadership for seven years and hinges in part on invoking trinity of the 'Father, Son and Holy Spirit' during the baptism." (Kaleem, p. 1 or 5). We see such matters of concern, that are presented within the pages of the Bible, and are clearly decipherable, whether technically by New Testament scholarship or simply by believers reading their own Bible, being reviewed for protocols and procedural issues constantly in the news. These matters are classic examples of the Christian believers across all denominations. Something as seemingly simple as baptism, which occurred as a outward demonstration of the new believers commitment to the gospel all through the letters of Paul and the Acts of the Apostles, being a matter of serious discussion even today after nearly 2000 years of Christian belief ... not that it doesn't need to be a part of the believers life commitment to Jesus, but that how the leader of the procedure conducts the "ceremony" and the words that are to be used is a matter of contention. The leaders of the long-standing Roman Catholic church are considering agreeing with the group of protestants if the verbal protocol is acceptable.

Another example of an issue of concern to a particular Christian believer is discussed in an article from "The American Journal of Biblical Theology." The author addresses the issue of greeting one another with a holy kiss. She states, "At the suggestion that the kiss is appropriate for use in the modern American church, I expect to encounter a fair degree of resistance. I believe the major contribution to this resistance is a concern regarding what kind of kiss is being suggested ... I contend that a proper understanding of Christian unity necessitates a true identification of believers as family." (Hunter, p. 6, 10) The very thought that she initiates is one that would be attended to by those who would counter with why are we trying to apply a conduct of greeting from 2000 years ago, that was obviously a matter of cultural tradition and acceptance and lay it flat on top of an American society with all its sexual issues being constantly in the news as problematic. On one hand there are constant efforts of local pastors, especially through sermons on marriage and efforts through the youth pastors, to address the need for extreme care in how one conducts oneself with the opposite sex. Now we have one person in a journal article making an issue out of the "holy kiss." The question to be asked in any and all cases where a matter of concern, no matter how sincere and genuine the proposal regarding a matter of Christian belief and practice, is just what is the positive, productive and most guaranteed successful way, strategy and protocol to gain an audience of informed and able respondees. If we were talking about he late 1890's in the United States, there were very few actual organized and standardized denominations. Names associated with Luthern, Baptist, Episcopal, Methodist and Church of Christ were quite common. This does not mean that there were not other groups who were around as long or even longer, but they remained somewhat random and fairly unrecognizable in the larger sense.

Latest Pew Research claims that the largest of Christian groups is Evangelical Christian, with Roman Catholic next. Probably unknown to even the average Christian adherent, the Mormon Church (Church of Jesus Christ of Latter Day Saints) is actually ranking fifth in Christian associated groups. In the Nashville, Tennessee area, for example, there are a number of groups with the word "Presbyterian" in their title name. One of those groups is called Cumberland Presbyterian. The name is taken from the fact that one of the central and major waterways through most of Tennessee is the Cumberland River … but also the access in early settlers time was called the Cumberland Gap through the Smokey Mountain range. Now, as simplistic as these facts may be about the naming of a fairly common and fairly good-sized and long-standing congregation of believers in the Southern part of the United States, it, nevertheless, represents what has happened over the years in the naming of any group of Christian believers. The simple fact of where they initiated their collection of first believers was a geographical reality and so Hence the name of the group was established. It might have begun with something as simple as a person visiting family from a long way off, and not knowing the details of just where to go in order to find their family, they ask a local resident for directions. They might simply say, "Can you tell me where the Smith family resides, here in this area near the river?" The person being asked will likely ask for some clarification, and the visitor might simply add they meet with the "river group of Christians." That is all the local resident needs and he or she points up the hill and describes a few details and the name of the Christian group is emphasized and eventually becomes common knowledge. As they continue to meet and grow, the name of the group in one way or the other becomes established. It might also be that as time passed and the local population grew, a minister of an established faith, with some sort of credentials ends up coming through the area, and meets some local folks and they offer him the opportunity to pastor the local flock.

If there were issues, conflicts and the such, that occurred over time, they were easily resolved Those folks simply starting another group meeting together and eventually establishing as a recognized group as well.

When one compares to today's current status of denominational issues, the matter becomes a Great deal more complex. Just using the United States and its 50 states and a few other jurisdictions, such as Puerto Rico, and Guam, and not so long ago, the Marshall Islands, the reasons for conflict just on the basis of local tradition, becomes even more complicated. For most Americans and immigrants today, it is not likely they remember the influx of Irish immigrants during one of the famine situations that occurred in Ireland around the turn of the last century. Obviously the Irish brought mainly Roman Catholic beliefs, and clearly their version of it. Since most established American families were leaning toward some form of protestant attachment, the large immigration of Irish was a bit too much, especially the tie with Roman Catholicism. As can be seen by the previous stats from Pew research, the presence of the Catholic church and its many colleges, schools, and other institutions is to be found in all areas of the United States.

When we simply address the content of the Bible, and particularly the New Testament teachings of Jesus and Paul and the other writers (James, John and the author of Jude and Hebrews) we find that every Christian group today has a particular leaning as to the relevancy of the content of these books and letters of the New Testament. Let us take a simple matter of whether the additional writings associated by some scholars of the New Testament with what is popularly referred to as the canon of the New Testament books, we find that most protestants accept the 27 current books as the official content of the New Covenant/Testament writings. But, one can find other examples of the Bible with additional books in both the New Testament section and the Old Testament section. A recent translation of the Bible, The Holman Christian Standard Bible, contains the classic listing of 39 books in the Old, from Genesis to Malachi, and 27 in the New Testament, from Matthew to Revelation. However, if one purchases or reviews a copy of The Roman Catholic bible, one finds a listing of "books" that are often referred to as the Apocrypha. There are versions, even of the apocrypha, with the Anglican, Orthodox and Catholic being the major ones that have developed over the centuries as per determinations by related scholars and textual experts who will advocate for the "legitimacy" of additional works.

One of the most significant works of recent time, that addresses the whole idea of "there might be other writings that are necessary parts of the Old or New Testament canons," is that written by Lee Strobel, entitled "The Case for the Real Jesus." In this remarkable book, the author, who was a major journalist for the Chicago Times, decided to use his investigatory skills to interview recognized scholars of the New Testament to determine for himself the validity of the life and work of Jesus Christ of Nazareth. As he pursued his quest to find out whether Jesus was a real person of history, and determine his own beliefs of Christianity, he found that there were many other advocated documents that contained alleged materials about Jesus and the teachings of the New Testament. (Strobel, p. 9-63) The more Mr. Strobel investigated, the more he ran into two basic elements of New Testament investigative efforts by the ones who ran the theological seminaries across the United States, in all the different denominational staffing. Some of the seminarial programs were within state universities or established major and long-term colleges and universities funded by private foundations. As he dealt with those seminary professors who had gained significant notoriety as a result participation in well-attended and well-publicized debate programs, and whose books on the various topics related to the apocryphal writings, he found that they either were determined to disenfranchise the entire Christian new covenant writings, or they were determined to investigate to establish the new covenant canon. As Mr. Strobel questioned and proposed to the particular scholars he chose to investigate, he became more and more struck by the differences in the manner in which both sides pursued their efforts. For those who stood for the effort to show that the whole idea of Christianity being something completely different for the many other religions that had been around as long, if not longer, he ran into an almost extremist attitude of trying to show the world of Christian believers that there are faults in their beliefs, their sources (texts, manuscripts, papyri, documents), and individuals of history supporting and proclaiming Christ's message.

In the text, "A Study of Early Christianity," the author tells us about how the original efforts to know Jesus are not as they are today. He states, "A genuinely biographical interest in Jesus is a peculiarly modern one. Prior to the middle of the eighteenth century, the Christian either accepted the four canonical Gospels as strictly accurate historical records or else neglected history altogether ... one of the chief problems has been the perspective of the modern scholar. Although this is a major problem in any historical writing, the study of the life of Jesus has been particularly plagued by it ... this being a number of anachronisms in biographies of Jesus ... usually in inoffensive ways, [editor: but nevertheless] speculations or subjective extensions of implications in the gospel texts." (Tyson, p. 341) If any of us were to go to the local library, or the much more inclined seminary library, one would find numerous books on the topic of the life, significance and overall impact of the man named Jesus of Nazareth. In these books, as alleged in the previous quote, there will be a huge variety of descriptions. These descriptions would include discussions on every topic imaginable as the person of Jesus is investigated. The discussions would address topics such as: where was he born and how can we be sure, since the Old Testament prophecies said one town, and yet he is called Jesus of Nazareth, instead of Jesus of Bethlehem (Micah 5: 2). Additional discussions would address whether or not he actually died on the Roman cross, whether or not that he was a legitimate prophet, whether or not he actually was resurrected from the dead. As any believer in Christianity knows, the Apostle Paul made it clear, that if Jesus of Nazareth had not resurrected from the dead, all that Believers are doing and claiming would be totally without value. He even went so far as to tell us that we would be the most foolish people of all (I Corinthians 15: 13-14).

Focusing on just the Bible itself brings about numerous conflicting issues for those who have investigated the legitimacy of the original texts of the Bible. For most believers today, the whole idea of actually checking into the history of the origin of the New Testament texts and how they eventually became what we know today as the canon of the New Testament ... the certified books and letters that are the genuine ones that represent the true teachings of Jesus, is something most have never actually done. Most individuals who go to a college supported by a Christian denomination, have only limited coursework that gets into actual personal student investigating the materials that brought about the writings of the New Testament and How it was established, settling on the final 27 books and letters. But, when one interviews average Christian adherents to the denominations that meet each Sunday and participate in the regular activities and services provided by the pastoral staff and support staff at the typical church, as to their understanding as to how the Bible, and specifically the New Testament originated, they are for the most part only able to provide a superficial answer.

There are numerous surveys by reputable organizations about the typical adult American Christian believer's understanding of the historical background information about the Bible's legitimacy, integrity, and continuing process of review as the archeological and technology of scientific investigations persist. They may know about the King James Version and even some of the more popular versions (Amplified, Revised Standard, English Standard and a few "Study" Bibles) but for them to realize that there are actually hundreds of English translations of the New Testament would more than likely bring them a shocked response. What the Bible says about unity would be a very similar matter. For any Christian believer to be asked about the importance of unity would most often bring a positive response ... "yes, it is important and it is something we need to work on." The whole concept of Christian unity is well attended and spoken of with a genuine concern for the work of the Gospel.

As noted earlier, when the work recently of the Billy Graham Association to promote a greater awareness of situation in the United States reached out to the people of the Christian churches to take their Christian duty more seriously and work harder to promote a unified effort in the preaching of the Gospel, there was a general acceptance of the need to do so. There were no negative responses to the implication that America needs to "wake up to the current moral and cultural situations in our nation." The average Christian believer is very much aware of the need to remain Godly in character and moral behavior, and will totally agree with such urgings, whether on a national scale as through the Billy Graham Association, or in their own weekly services, well-spoken by the local pastor or special invited speaker as a guest from some evangelistic association may be heard. The speakers often speak of the need to present the good news of Jesus in as effective a way as possible, as new methods and upgraded techniques are tried and proven to be successful. In today's church groups an ongoing adjustment is being continually made to successfully use the increased and readily effective technological devices and procedures. The whole world of the Bible has been brought to the individual cell phone, with the programs that allow the Bible to be read on the screens of those phones even while listening to music and participating in their regular work. The availability of the Scriptures is at an all-time high, especially in the United States. The availability of scripture in so many newer translations has made it easier for many to read the text of scripture. There are chronological Bibles, and Bibles that have been divided up to provide a daily reading over a year's period. For the average American, and for that matter, the average Westerner (North and

South America, Australia, Europe and Russia, and much of India and some other economically better off nations), the Bible is at their beck and call. One would think the increased availability and easy costs and purchase circumstances, as well as organizations like the American Bible Society and Gideons, have done incredible work in the overall process of distributing the Word of God, as represented in the Old and New Covenant works.

John Haley authored the text, "Alleged Discrepancies of the Bible," in which he addresses the many efforts of scholars, denominations and simply individuals wanting to discredit the Bible. One example he lists is one that has been generally legitimized due to the fact of the lack of any credible early documents of the New Testament that have this portion of I John in those earliest documents. In I John 5: 7 is refers to a complimentary analogy of the previous verse which lists the blood of Christ, the water of baptism and the Spirit of God. The author states the following regarding this particular verse: "I John is a spurious passage. It is found in no Greek manuscript before the fifteenth or sixteenth century, and in no early version. It is rejected by Alford, Abbot, Bleek … and most modern critics." (Haley, p. 60) Now we can see what a particular verse, to be found in the King James Version (which was the main English translation available for many centuries) has impacted the beliefs of Christians for many years. It has not been unusual at all for the average pastor/minister of the faith to use this verse to substantiate the belief in the Trinity doctrine. Again, the problem is hugely significant, not in the sense of bringing any kind of degradation on the belief in the Trinity God, but in the light of the basic need to teach and empower the local congregants (Christian believers) in the research of the truths of the Bible and its historical development. When the average Christian goes about his or her daily duties, with the opportunities at work, in the neighborhood or at the mall to present the good news message and uses a passage like I John 5 to assure that Jesus is God like the Father is God and the Holy Spirit is the Power of God, and the three are one God, and the new believer runs across an updated Bible version with the spurious passage notation, what does that do to the legitimacy of Gospel presentation? If there is truly unity in the Church across the board, then such matters of non-credible citings in scripture, are a lot less likely to occur. As mentioned earlier in this paper, the story of the adulterous woman being brought to Jesus to be confronted with the Old Testament law of stoning the adulterous person, and the way in which it shows the very truth of the compassion, and forgiveness of God, in Jesus' death and sacrifice, it is so hard to realize that it is not a credible portion of the New Testament texts. It is simply not found in the earliest documents. (Strobel, p. 90-91) So what does this kind of inaccurate rendering of the scriptures do to our effort to bring unity in the Church? One can certainly speculate on the opportunists outside the church, taking full advantage of such apparently misleading presentation. There are those of the more uneducated and simple people, just as convicted of sin and willing to live for Christ as the well-informed and educated Christians with significant background in the history of the church and the documents of the Bible books and letters, who will continue to believe what is in the King James Version as the wholly, and holy, word of God. For anyone to confront them with such citings in scripture that are not accurate reflection of the earliest documents of Bible books and letters of the New Covenant, would only create a stand-off of often major proportions, further dividing the local churches in the particular location or area. These are representative of issues of the Bible and its comprehension, and then, presentation (teaching and preaching) to the average believer. When a new minister or pastor comes into a local congregation in modern times, often it is the duty of the group of individuals that make up a oversight committee to choose that person. Unlike that situation, is the more common situation today, especially in the

United States, to have a small group of folks decide that they no longer wish to attend a particular congregation. They decide that one of them is a good selection for leading them. As time goes on the group appreciates the teaching skills of that person, and the group decides to "ordain" that person as their pastor. So, another group of Christian believers begins. The ability of the "pastor/leader" to provide the necessary teachings on what it means to be a Christian can range from "okay" to "just enough" to "taking them off into some fringe areas" that create a peculiarity for their way to conduct, live and present their beliefs to others.

One of the major issues in the United States, and now affecting various Western nations and those nations influenced by these economically advanced groups of nations, is the core belief that each person has the right to believe as they choose. It is not uncommon for individuals of knowledge regarding personal rights and freedoms to proclaim the right of a group or individual to speak to any position on any issue. This is advocated even though it has the potential to create confusion, unrest and even various degrees of outright rebellion against Established government of leadership of a recognized/established organization. This freedom of speech fosters and environment that definitely affects the Christian groups, especially within them among the actual Christian believers. So if a new pastor wants to begin using a new translation of the Bible which gives a little different slant of such rather simple matters of whether a woman can be ordained as a minister (addressing Paul's directives in I Timothy, chapter 2, verses 9 – 15), it can create division in that group, as they may have taken those admonitions of Paul as a clear statement of not ordaining women, and now this new pastor is suggesting something quite different. The problem is often a case of just how well are the congregation of believers taught in the weekly sermons and bible studies, and advised on good Christian teaching books that can be studied and read on their own. When knowledge of

God's word is well-rooted and the believers are well-grounded, then new teaching can be Screened and reviewed and searched out for the legitimacy and significance of the teaching. When the initial writers of the New Testament completed what they wrote, it was a long time before the teachings, and content of that which gave direction on living the Christian life, was available in printed form for regular re-reading and direct teaching from the texts. For many years after even the original texts were completed, the brothers and sisters of the Lord were teaching from oral re-teaching and passing on "oral tradition." When they would meet in the homes of the local Christian believers, the leaders would teach from what they had been taught by the apostles and evangelists originally, and then the works of Paul, James, Mark John, Jude, Matthew and Luke, were passed on orally for the most part until copies and re-writings were made available. Of course, the exact sequence of how the earliest ones (parchments, scrolls, etc.) we have today of the New Testament texts became available can only be historically established based on the writings of early Christian leaders who spoke in their messages and remembrances of the apostles, as well as wrote their own letters both quoting and stating in their own words what they remembered to be the core teachings of Jesus and Paul and others. The wonderful archeological and scholarly positive result has been a huge recovery of the oldest documents in writing, both Greek, Aramaic, and other local languages from that time of the first and second centuries that corroborate the actual core teachings and full renderings of each of the New Testament canon texts. A scientific and ethical review of all these ancient copies of the texts have brought about a remarkably reliable and accurate rendering of the each of the letters, books and messages of the New Testament.

Does this mean that all the churches, denominations and other Christian groups and associations agree on the actual texts? No. Does it mean that all these Christian groups and their scholarly experts, especially those from the seminaries and recognized colleges and universities that study the ancient writings come to common ground on what these established texts actually teach? No. The many translations of the New Testament in particular (as well as the whole Bible) have made the gospel message available, but it has not caused a gradual and consistent coming together in a grand spectacle of unity within the entirety of the Christian Church Universal. There are countless interpretations of so many doctrines and beliefs ... even within a single denomination ... often occurring at one of their national annual conventions. These are times for lectures and presentations, often by popular authors and scholars who have addressed a particular issue and a recently published book/text. It is not uncommon for a particular presenter and/or writer/author to state something within a speech or presentation, whether at a general conference setting or in one of the many workshops, side meetings during the convention, to bring up a variation of a topic long held sacrosanct over the length of time this particular Christian group has been organized. This can often become a matter of discussion and eventual review by the upper authorities of the organization/association of Christian believers. This can lead to further investigation of the specifics of the different aspects and legitimacy of the "facts" that were presented. The larger the Christian group and the extent of its geographical boundaries can add significantly to the probabilities of the possible differences to the promoted and taught policies, doctrinal interpretations peculiar to this group, and therefore make it all the more difficult to stay on top of possible incorrect teachings.

The correct and usually intentional effort on the part of the authorities who must investigate the alleged contradiction to current belief and long-held interpretation of scripture, is to take the time to meet with those making the assertions and striving to bring a collective understanding so that the presentation and the established doctrines can be rectified.

A recent 2013 event was held to promote unity. According to the article in the Anglican Journal, "A week of Prayer for Christian Unity (this year from Jan. 18-25, 2013) is celebrated by over two billion Christians world-wide ... this year's theme is 'What does God require of us? (Micah 6: 6-8) What the Lord does require of you, but to do justice, to love kindness, and work Humbly with your God.'" "A sampling of WofPforCU celebrations across Canada ... bishop gave Lecture on 'How Communion Changes Ecumenism.'" ... a collaboration service will be conducted by Catholic, Baptist, United Church of Canada, Presbyterian and Evangelical Lutheran pastors." (Sison, p. 1 of 1)

Bringing peace among believers according to the Bible, must occur by those who have made a true commitment to Jesus as Lord and Savior. The practice of religion, for the sake of simply joining an organization that seems to have a good heart and does "good things," is not the core value of the successful implementation of the Bible and what is taught in the New Testament for the successful unification of believers. Just because people come together and attend times of gathering and share speeches on how their own association of Christian adherents is striving to promote unity does not address the real causes of creating Godly unity in the Body of Christ. The Bible teaches in the New Testament that the individual Christian has got to read and study the Bible on a personal basis, to gain the mind of God and Christ. It is only when the Word of God, as Jesus said, "I am the way, the truth and the life, no one comes to the Father but through me." (John 14: 6-7) It is the personal relationship with Jesus that initiates the capacity and desire on the part of the individual believer to know the truth about all aspects of the Kingdom of God. Since there is one Kingdom, and Jesus is the King of that kingdom, it is only logical that the spirit of unity is critical for the individual Christian to savor, enlist, practice and live by. By studying the very Word of God, knowing that John wrote in the first chapter of the Gospel of John that Jesus is the Word, and the Word is with God and the Word of God, it only follows that being thoroughly knowledgeable about the Word will enable the believer to be a producer and promoter of unity. As the word of God is studied and read, and studied and read over time, the Christian becomes deeply rooted in the whys and hows of unity in Christ. Unity is going to be a lifetime effort, refining through all the experiences of living God's way through each and every day, with the trials, opportunities, blessings and experiences of living as a child of God and a disciple of Jesus. As one interrelates with fellow believers, it becomes more and more obvious that the qualities of unity enhance and promote the preparation for the Kingdom. Just as Jesus in his earthly existence (all God and all man), focused on promoting every aspect of the Kingdom, through his own study of the Word as he learned it from his parents, the local synagogue and the teachings of the Sabbath from the rabbis and priests, so each of those who claim the relationship with God through Jesus are to seek the Kingdom of God first and His righteousness (Matthew 6: 33-34). When the priorities are straight and the life of the believer is founded on every word of God, the eventual result will always be an attitude that promotes cooperation, working together, being patient and attentive to the needs of others, and a willingness to work things out.

Yet, today as one would follow along through the various denominational services and bible studies, from Lutheran to Church of Christ to Roman Catholic to Southern Baptist and even Church of Jesus Christ of Latter Day Saints, any topic being presented will certainly have a generic commonality, whether who Jesus is or how the Bible came about. But just the slightest further bit of listening and reading of the notes from the leader's presentation, there will be variations. For example, in one congregation the subject of ladies leading in the local congergation will go to passages like I Timothy 2: 9-15, and declare the benefit of leaving the leading of the brethren to the men of the group of believers … asking such questions as, "Which of the twelve apostles was a woman?" In the next congregation, taking a more "liberal" interpretation will support the ordination of a young lady who has just graduated from a seminary with a degree in ministry. That leadership will be sure to show that it was the cultural issues of the day in which Paul and all around the Mediterranean area lived that kept women out of leadership roles. Yet, in the next congregation/denomination the pastor or priest will point to the wonderful work of the congregational lady members who have taken leadership roles and served with excellence … avoiding the biblical arguments altogether.

One can only project in one's mind what the massive worldwide conference of gaining unity across all Christian groups would be like. Taking a careful and organized approach, the overseers would use the many techniques for effective mediation. Daniel Bowling's book, "Bringing Peace into the Room," gives us an incite as to the approach that could be taken: "(Paradoxes in Mediation) One of the mediator's principal tasks is to win the trust of parties. From the first moments of their involvement with the parties or their counsel, the mediator seeks to convince them that she will be fair and evenhanded. In theory, transparency—candor by the mediator about the process and the mediator's role in it—enhances such trust … yet there are aspects of the mediator's work that, according to some, involve deception and manipulation." (Bowling, p. 173). Furlong, in his text, "The Conflict Resolution Toolbox," tells us that the motives and intentions of the parties involved are critical. He states, among other comments on the topic, "perceptions are influenced mostly by two factors: information and preconception.. still, attributions can be changed." (Furlong, p. 137)

As we continue to oversee this huge congregation of leaders and representatives of all the many Christian groups from all over the world, we began to see what Robert Welch addresses in his book, "Church Administration: Creating Efficiency for Effective Ministry." His concern in this part of the text is the issues of leadership taking advantage of the situation. He states: ... "we wil discuss four dysfunctional (leadership) styles that are prevalent in the Church today ... the Showman: has an inflated view of their leadership position and ability ... the Doubting Thomas: has not developed the ability to rely upon those they lead ... The Monk: this is an individualist, doing his role with no interaction with others in the congregation ... The Control Freak: assures that the organization functions exactly as this leader dictates." (Welch, p. 42-44).

Obviously the Bible demands a servant leader and that any convention of world Christian leadership to address the need and the means to the end of succeeding with Unity in the Church Universal will require a number of changes and modifications in how the groups of Christians teach, preach, live and promote the Gospel message of peace, hope, salvation and relationship with God and the other Christians that is based on oneness in Christ.

# CONCLUSION

# The Strategies and Means
# to Church Unity

As this incredibly critical core value to the basic principles of Christian belief is reviewed and finalized, it is essential to the entirety of this paper (book) that the overall history of the church, in the briefest of terms is described.

It began on the Day of Pentecost after the Spring-time death and resurrection of Jesus Christ of Nazareth was completed. His death was predicted by himself on many occasions as he worked his three and one-half year ministry with his disciples (John 12: 27, for example). They were at all points and times immediately against it or acted as if they did not understand the need for his sacrifice.

This is attributable to various reasonings: they wanted him to be the Messiah of the Old Testament prophecies that would take Israel out of bondage (Daniel 9, for example), and there was the sense of desire to protect Jesus who was such a remarkable prophet at the least, and another reason was the remarkable overall impact of Jesus on all the peoples of the area, from the Samaritans, to the Roman guards, to the Leaders of the Jews as they failed to make him look deficit in any way as they tried to nail him in front of the crowds with pre-prepared questions, devised by their best "lawyers."

Yet through all of this public, and within the disciples/followers context, Jesus remained wholly committed to proclaiming the love of God the Father for all mankind. This profound focus on all of humanity (as illustrated with the 'woman at the well' in Samaria), created a core resonance in his teachings that founded them all on a unifying theme of salvation for all. If all humanity were to become the children of God, and this was even well-taught in the works of the prophets as they were told to proclaim the intent of God's purpose for even the heathen and non-Israelites (the example of the harlot woman (Joshua 2: 2) were to look forward to a time of salvation for all. God's overall purpose was began in the Garden of Eden with non-Israelite Adam and Eve. His intent was to provide the blessing of fellowship with them through a life of eternal blessing and learning. The problem was in giving them their potential opportunity they were also given the gift of "free will." They were not robots. They were not angels as the case was for all those attending the throne of God throughout eternity past. And just as the book of Hebrews tells us that Jesus was tested in all things as any human was (Heb. 5: 7-10), so the whole idea of cooperation, obedience, a desire to become wholly involved in the work of the Eternal God was presented to the first humans, and they ultimately chose disunity, and going their own way, the way that leads to death and not anything close to eternal life. The coming of the Messiah was heralded at the highest levels as declared in the early portions of the Gospels, especially as described in the Gospel of Luke (Luke 2: 8-14). Jesus worked to be in unity with the Father from the very beginning, as evidenced by his commitment to being baptized by John (his cousin) and following all the directives the Father God gave him. So, as Jesus realized the immediacy of his actual physical/mortal death, he focused on the need for remaining in complete compliance with the Father and the salvation plan for everyone. His prayer in John 17 focuses on a number of unity issues. First of all was his continued, and never lost, desire to be at one with the Father, and in turn, to make the disciples (the ones the Father had given him ... see John 6:44, 65) one with him and the Father. Oneness declares all of the characteristics of cooperation and avoidance of anything that undermines, distracts, preoccupies with other things, or makes secondary. So, again, we see a person whose focus and whole being is targeted on the goals, vision and multiple objectives of the Father. In the process of reaching out to both the disciples who became the apostles, and the massive groups of followers, he was constantly aware of the needs that cause anyone to lose focus ... illness, deformities, injuries and disease. The other main issue appeared to be various issues related to food and employment for providing financial capacity for the needs of each day. He healed and gave direction for what was needed to be successful getting along with others and even those who were determined to subjugate them ... the Roman conquerors. In all that Jesus taught and demonstrated, he focused the attention of others on the fact that God the Father was the source of all good things and worked constantly to help them believe in God and his plan for all mankind. As the time neared for his sacrificial death, he remained committed to moving toward the location for it to take place ... he moved toward Jerusalem. As Jesus continued his ministry, even to the very end, he attended to others, such as the ladies that watched him carry the cross to his place of crucifixion ... he encouraged them: his mother and John at his cross, and those ladies (John 19: 26-27, Luke 23: 27-31). All of his words, work and example presented the value and need for unity in all that is to be done for the Kingdom.

Now that we have seen and been reminded of the life work of Jesus, we can see more clearly the words of the apostles and other followers who wrote to the believers in the various cities around the Mediterranean. Paul the Apostle in particular along with John wrote of the love of God, both as directed to each and every human being, and the admonition to serve others with that same love (Romans 13: 8 and I John 4: 7-21). As mentioned earlier in this book, Jesus gave immediate confirmation to the leader of the Jews who asked him what was the most important commandment ... to love God and your neighbor as yourself. This was the same admonition that Paul gave to the church at Ephesus regarding the relationship of husband to wife and wife to husband. The parallel to the workings of the Church as the Body of Christ was a great application of the need for unity at even the basic of relationships (Ephesians 5: 22-33). So what is the bottom line for unity? It begins on the personal level, as one gives their life to God through accepting Jesus Christ as Lord and Savior. One must be born-again by the Spirit of God enabling the believer to exercise the power of God to overcome the pulls of the flesh. That spirit of oneness with God is demonstrated by what Paul calls the fruits of the Spirit. In Galatians 5: 16 and following to the end of the chapter, Paul teaches the need to walk in the Spirit and overcome the desires of the flesh. For each believer there is the internal power of God in us to demonstrate the character of one of God's children: " ...love, joy, peace, patience, kindness, goodness, faithfulness, gentleness, self-control ..." It is taught that when each Christian believer allows God by his Spirit to enforce the life of one born into the Kingdom of God, his or her life will promote and advocate unity in all they do. Exercising these actions of personal behavior sets up the environment to create a unifying desire in all the believers with which one fellowships in the congregation. Out of that empowerment must radiate a true desire for unity in all that one says, does and promotes.

Obviously, the individual believer must be taught the ways of unity. As the pastors of churches conduct the weekly services and bible studies, it is critical that they teach how the way of unity can be developed and maintained and made more effectively a part of all the Christian community does as a witness throughout their community, especially to those who have yet to come to a relationship with Jesus. The purpose and benefits of unity must be admonished and taught as a regular part of all that pastors, teachers and leaders present to the Christian group. For many pastors/ leaders/ministers the focus on unity across Christianity is a hard to do thing, because they are so preoccupied with the teaching needed to keep their own group of believers in their congregation targeted on what their congregation is needing to do. It is not easy to give attention to the believing Christians in all other groups and locations around the state, nation and area of the world.

Through missionaries supported by local congregations and associations of Christian believers, new believers are brought into the Body of Christ all over the world, and this continues on a very large scale to this very day. However, the very fact of the huge distances between the new believers and the ones supporting the missions effort, make the promotion of unity quite a difficult thing. It is more of a cultural and language issue, as the way the new believers will be able to live their lives will not necessarily follow the ways of the supporting churches who send out the missionaries. However, the power of the Holy Spirit, when the new believers sincerely request the blessings of God, will, according to the Word of God, bring the necessary provisions to empower and create the opportunities for maturing in Christ. This obviously will develop the fruit of the Spirit, if requested and daily solicited from God that will create an atmosphere of oneness in Christ.

*So, unity must be based and founded on the born-again spirit from the time of personal salvation.* As each Christian brother and sister comes to the saving knowledge of Jesus Christ, and accepts the gospel by faith, then the cooperative spirit of unity is invested in not only the individual, but into the group of Christian believers. As Jesus worked with his disciples (the apostles to be, as well as the larger group of followers), he pointed them to the Father as the source of all good things. His teachings like the "Beatitudes," gave the multitudes and the selected apostles the knowledge of what God's family, the Body of Christ (yet to be established at Pentecost), was to be ... a family of brothers and sisters with Jesus as the Elder Brother and Savior/Lord. For there to be unity in the Church, with all the uniqueness of the individual Christian, and the influence of culture, race, and previous life, with its acceptances in behavior, morality, priorities and experiences, there must be a serious and ongoing teaching by the servant leaders of the group as to God's priorities of behavior: patience, acceptance, kindness, forgiveness and a willingness to learn and develop respect for others. This means avoidance of jealousy, envy, over-reaction to perceived social indifferences, and a whole slew of issues that make the one Christian brother, especially one who is new to the faith, not feel an integral part of the family of believers. Too often the things one values and gives priority too, even in the recreational side of one's life, can be minimized by others, simply by ignoring it. So many aspects of growing in Christ need to be taught, experienced and given opportunity for guided improvement. As the individuals and the congregation matures, it becomes obvious that certain well-held traditions and/or practices need to be eliminated, based on better understanding of the biblical study, or at least, modified in the positive direction. For example, if the congregation comes to believe that merely sprinkling water over the head of a new believer is not what the Bible actually teaches, both by example in such books as the Acts of the Apostles, but also by the picture of baptism as a representation of going into the grave (as Christ did) and coming up out of the water (Romans 6). But, we would always have to be careful that we don't make unity a case of "uniformity." Simply because men are men and women are women, and each human being is different (even the alleged identical twins) ...

unique, God expects each to be a part of the Body of Christ (the one Church, as Christ has only one body) and do that which that part does to make it all work successfully. The hand cannot do the work of the nose, as Paul the Apostle so aptly explained. (I Cor. 12)

What might some of the obstacles be to undermine even the most desired and well-intentioned efforts for unity? Consider the issue of alcoholic beverages. As long as one believer believes that the bottle of wine is the "tool of the devil," the chances for fellowship with another believer (who may have actually had to give up drinking alcohol due to a problem with excessive drinking binges), who sees alcohol as not the problem, but the over indulgence as the problem. Too often each person who declares their adherence to the Gospel of Christ, is unwilling to acknowledge their closely held beliefs and practices as simply "their own beliefs" that may be perfectly moral and non-contradictory to the Christian life, but they are not based on the teachings of the New Testament. For example, if one has taken the Old Testament admonitions to not eat pork to heart, and ends up attending a church in the South that has barbeques focused on pork ribs, that will be a personal problem. Such matters can be taken to a much higher level of impact, if that person is a minister and was hired to be the new pastor of that church in the South. When a Christian runs up against that which is beginning to undermine their own efforts to promote unity in the church, it is critical that they learn the expert and loving methods of doing their own Bible study and gaining the input of their pastors or even good friends in the fellowship, which is what a fellowship is for, so they can weigh the facts and gain the techniques, strategies and practices that will empower them to overcome any and all obstacles to unity of the faith.

*So why is there not unity of the Church Universal?* It is a simple matter of their being so many obstacles to it having occurred throughout the past two thousand years. With over 7,000 languages on planet Earth at the present time, according to Wycliffe Bible Translators (whose whole goal is to complete at least the New Testament translations for any languages yet to have it, by the year 2020), one can readily see that teaching the Gospel message is of itself a major task, that is only recently beginning to be seen as possible across all the 195 nations of the present world. Beyond the issue of languages, is the huge variety of cultures, often associated with the different language situation. We are also confronted with the governance of our lives by the national authorities. Especially in the Western nations, there are so many interferences to accomplishing unity in being able to join together in a simplified way. The impact of those functioning in the legal professions creates complications as well.

However, the Bible is quite clear that achieving unity of the faith is a critical issue, and cannot be ignored, except to the detriment of our own personal and collective relationship with God the Father through the work of salvation in Jesus by the power of the Holy Spirit.

The steps to unity of the faith, bringing about the universal church, the one body of Christ, are based on the following:

1. Each believer must be a born-again follower of Jesus Christ (have the Spirit of God)
2. Each believer must be committed to promoting unity within the local congregation and across all groups of true believers (Christians, who believe in Jesus as Savior)
3. Each Christian group must be taught the value, the effective practices and the intent and benefits of unity in all quarters of the church around the world.
4. The leaders of the Christian groups have got to have a plan, vision and practice of teaching unity of the faith (the value of being and critical teachings of Jesus) as an integral part of all that is taught to the brothers and sisters of the faith.

5. The people who are in positions of leadership must be grounded and committed to teaching the members of the group the strategies and practices that promote unity in their relationships with other believers of other Christian groups. They must teach the believers how to overcome the typical obstacles that can readily interfere with any effort to be in unity … often this includes cultural differences, national origins, traditions (even within families and communities), and language issues.

6. Established Christian organizations have got to take on the task of planning for ways to get past the long-time established practice of separate denomination and association groups that intentionally compete for status and recognition among the Christian world of believers. Each organization must be established based on the keys to unity Of the faith.

7. A great deal of earnest and effective prayer of righteous believers and leaders of the Christian faith must be made to the Great Eternal Father God in the Name of the Lord and Savior Jesus Christ to begin to bring the Unity of the Faith about by the miracle of the Power of the Holy Spirit of God creating a deeply rooted heart of servant leadership in each and every believer … a willingness to repent of selfish and long-held traditions that have undermined unity and have created separations and disunity across the board.

Ultimately, the unity of the Body of Christ will be culminated at the return of Jesus at the second-coming of Christ Jesus. At that time, with Jesus no longer a visually abstract concept, but a powerful eternal Son of God, King of all Creation, the nations of the world will also become unified, by the power of God and his angels, with the newly immortalized believers made eternal with the family of God forever. We must see the ultimate vision for unity.

# BIBLIOGRAPHY

## References and Cited Notations

Alessandra, Tony, Hunsaker, Phil. Communicating at Work. Simon and Schuster: New York, 1993, p.98.

> "Rather than depending on negotiation or compromise, collaboration relies on creative problem-solving to identify solutions that will meet the needs of all parties. There are four basic components of collaboration: understanding and respecting the goals and objectives of each of the parties, assertiveness, creative problem-solving, and confrontation."

Akers, John & Armstrong, John (editors). This We Believe. Zondervan Publishing House: Grand Rapids, 2000, p. 240.

> "The Gospel is the only Gospel: there is no other; and to change its substance is to pervert and indeed destroy it ... all Christians are called to unity in love and unity in truth. As evangelicals who derive our very name from the Gospel, we celebrate this great good news of God's saving work in Jesus

Christ as the true bond of Christian unity, whether among organized churches and denominations or in the many transdenominational cooperative enterprises of Christians together.

Acts 4: 32. "Acts of the Apostles," The New Testament: Holman Christian Standard Bible. 95 A.D., p. 1868.

"Now the large group of those who believed were of one heart and mind, and no one said that any of his possessions was his own, but instead they held everything in common."

Bacheller, Irving. A Man for the Ages. Grosset and Dunlap Publishers: New York, 1919, p. 410.

"The Republican State Convention had endorsed him for the United States Senate. It was then that he wrote on envelopes and scraps of paper at odd moments, when his mind was off duty, the speech beginning: 'a house divided against itself must fall. Our government can not long endure part slave and part free.'"

Barker, Kenneth & Kohlenberger, John III. Zondervan NIV New Testament Commentary, Vol. 2, p. 769.

"The ultimate end in view is the attainment of completeness in Christ. 'We all' clearly includes all believers, but not all people. In verse 3 'unity of the Spirit' is a gift to be guarded; here 'unity in the faith' is a goal to be reached. Such a realization of unity will arise from an increasing knowledge of Christ as the Son of God in corporate as well as in personal experience."

Batterson, Mark. PRIMAL. Multnomah Books: Colorado Springs, Colorado, 2009, p. 153.

"None of us can imagine what God is capable of. Which means none of us can imagine what we're capable of if we give God control of our lives. His power sets off a chain reaction. And with His energy at work within us, there is nothing we can't do ... but many of never flip the switch. We never receive the power He promised. And without His power, we become nothing more than theological Christians ... without His power At work within us, we cannot accomplish His purposes."

Baxter, J. Sidlow. Explore the Book. Zondervan: Grand Rapids, 1966, p. 176

"...and that during the present age an elect people, the Church, should be gathered out, irrespective of nationality—an elect people who should be brought collectively into an intimate union of life and love and eternal glory with Him ... (Eph. 3-4)"

Becker, Penny Edgell. Congregations in Conflict: Cultural Models of Local Religious Life. Cambridge University Press: 1999, p. 87.

"If families have homes, families also avoid politics and other controversial issues, or at least middle-class families do ... implying that groups (in this case, congregations) with a close family-like attachment suppress disagreement and avoid debate ... one pastor found out how difficult it was to spark public discussion of social issues in his family congregation ... when asked what his congregation's position was on abortion or homosexuality, they reported no official stand ..."

Benson, Clarence H. and Morgan, Robert J. Exploring Theology. Crossway Books: Wheaton, Illinois, 2007, p. 173.

"The Christians united not only as a church, but as a family. Many Jewish converts were ostracized by their families and friends; so the Christians helped and encouraged one another. Their mutual faith in the Messiah bound them together as a group. The Holy Spirit worked mightily as a result of their unity ... They recognized their vital need for fellowship and remained steadfast in it. If the members had stopped to criticize, no doubt they would have found faults in each other. Instead, they were quick to see their own failures, but slow to criticize others."

Boulton, Wayne G., Kennedy, Thomas D., Verhey, Allen. From Christ to the World. Eerdmans Publishing Company: Grand Rapids, 1994, p. 305.

"Throughout its early period, Christianity seems to have been most appealing precisely to those marginal groups that were not engaged in landholding, in agricultural production, or in the service of rulers ... in brief, Christianity has been linked from its inception to urbanized people involved in producing and trading ... Corporations have created more wealth than most of humankind can imagine."

Bowling, Daniel. Bringing Peace into the Room. Jossey-Bass: San Francisco, 2003, p. 173.

From the first moments of her involvement with the parties or their arguments the mediator seeks to convince them that she will be fair and evenhanded. In theory, transparency—candor by the mediator about the process and mediator's role in it— enhances such trust ... yet there are aspects of the mediator's work that, according to some, involve deception and manipulation."

Carson, Dr. Ben. One Nation. Penguin Group Random House: New York, 2014, p. 174-175.

"Deep Division: Because of our neglect of the Constitution, it has been a while since the people of America could agree on a national vision. Perhaps the last time was toward the end of the Cold War when our unity and strength radically changed the world's power structure for the better."

Cathon, Brother. "Early Church History," (Mt. Juliet, TN Church of Christ), 2014, p. 1 of 2.

"The third question of interest is why the split caused by the liberal element was so late in making its influence felt here. The movement started in the 1800's and the split was was complete by 1906, yet it was evidently 1915 before the brethren became alarmed ... Bro. Elam's states 'this property is to be used only for a House of Worship for a congregation of the Church of Christ. It is a condition of this conveyance (the deed) without which it would not be made, that the use of instrumental music in the worship at all times be forbidden ... '"

Cleveland, Christina. Disunity in Christ. Intervarsity Christian Fellowship: Madison, Wisconsin, 2013, p. 1 of 3.

"Cleveland takes a different tack and examines many of the social factors that inhibit the church's desire for unity ... not discounting the theological issues, while challenging her readers to examine biases and presuppositions that govern the way they interact with the 'other.'"

Coffee, Blake. "Big Business and Big Churches," http://fiveprinciples.net, 2014, p. 1 of 3.

"Biblical scholar, Dr. Richard Halverson, has said, "When the Greeks got the gospel, they turned it into a philosophy; when the Romans got it, they turned it into a government; when the Europeans got it, they turned it into a culture, and when the Americans got it, they turned it into a business."

"Here are some not-so-discreet differences between corporate processes and Spiritual processes ... 1. Business casts a vision of what it wants to accomplish and then sets out to gather resources to accomplish it ... the church we should allow God to show us by using the human resources we already have. 2. Business starts with incorporating documents and then allows those documents to determine how it acts ... the church only uses documents to comply with the public governing agencies ..."

Davis, John Jefferson. Evangelical Ethics. Presbyterian and Reformed Publishing Co.: Phillipsburg, New Jersey, 2004, p. 263.

"Since Lynn White, a professor of history at UCLA wrote: 'Our present science and our present technology are so tinctured with orthodox Christian arrogance toward nature ... ' Is it really the case that the Bible teaches that nature exists only to serve man?"

Drucker, Peter F. The Essential Drucker. Harper Collins Publishers: New York, 2001, p. 215

"In a hospital, for instance—perhaps the most complex of the modern knowledge organizations—nurses, dieticians, physical therapists, medical and X-ray technicians, pharmacologists, pathologists, and a host of other health-related professionals have control by anyone. And yet they have to work together for a common end and in line with a general plan of action: the doctor's prescription for treatment ... each of these professionals has to keep all the others informed according to a specific situation, the condition, and the need of an individual patient."

Durgan, M. Erk. Geometric Generalization of the Structure of Nature: Abstract Principles. www.unitytheory.info/philosophy, 2009, Chapter 9, p. 1 of 4.

"Principles of mathematics, geometry, etc. can be proved logically. However, the logical reasoning of the causality and unity is more problematic … the concept of unity goes much beyond that, since parts of the wholeness cannot observe the wholeness as a whole. (Indeed, if these concepts … of causality and unity … are deeply examined, it might be deduced that these concepts include logical arguments within themselves as to why they are a priori concepts."

Eck, Donna. Council on Christian Unity. "Understanding Unity I a Religiously Diverse World," No. 2, 2003, p. 1 of 4.

"Christian unity is the theme of the ecumenical movement. The modern ecumenical movement began in the wake of World War II as Christians came together from all sides of a war-torn world to affirm a common commitment. This, after centuries of fission and separation. This, after years of the horror of war. The old scars of Europe, the legacies of colonialism, and the denominational extravaganza of the United States have not made this work easy … they are not just issues of Christian unity, but of human unity and human relationship in a world fractured by religious devision."

Editor. Number Of.net. http://www.numberof.net/number-of-christiandenominations, Aug. 2014, p. 1 of 3.

"There are about 34,000 different Christian groups in the world since AD 30 … this According to the World Christian Encyclopedia published in 2001 … 1200 different Christian denominations exist in the United States alone … some have established 8 mega-groups, namely Roman Catholic, Eastern Orthodoxy, Oriental Orthodoxy, Assyrian Churches, Protestantism, Restorationism, Anglican Communicants, Pentecostal, and others."

Editor. Pew Research: Religion and Public Life Project. http://religions.pewform.org, Aug. 2014, p. 1 of 10.

"The largest Christian group is Evangelical Christian, with Roman Catholic next. They represent 32 percent of population. Mormon make up the 5th largest group in the U.S.A."

Editor. Pew Research: Forum on Religion and Public Life. http://religions.perforum.org/reports/ Dec. 2013, p. 1 of 3.

"78.4 percent of U.S. citizens connect to Christian religion. Foreign born Christian adherents are two to one Catholic over Protestant. The survey finds that constant movement characterizes the American religious marketplace, as every major

religious group is simultaneously gaining and
losing adherents."

Editor. http://www.challies.com. Twelve Ways to Preserve
Christian Unity, July 2013, p. 1 of 5.

"Spend more time considering evidence of grace
that the sins of others. Spiritual safety comes
through spiritual unity ... when one isolates
oneself by disrupting or denying unity that one is
most at risk. Meditate on God's many commands
to love one another (i.e., Jn. 15: 12, I Jn. 4: 7, I
Pet. 1: 22). Focus on on the areas of agreement
than on those of disagreement. Remember that
God is a God of peace ... making our peace with
God obligates making peace with others. Preach
peace to yourself, as God has forgiven you, be
more tolerant of others. Dwell on the admonition
in Ps. 133: 1 ... how good and pleasant it is for
brothers to dwell together in unity. Remind
oneself of the cost to the church when disunity
is perpetuated ... Satan wins. Take the initiative
to promote unity on your own, not waiting for
others to start it or promote it ... be an instigator
with joy and love. Let God's word be the judge,
so one can focus on working together rather
than scrutinizing the work and motivations of
others. Focus on self-judging my own actions and
motivations in the light of God's word rather than
that of brothers. Pursue humility to promote the
attitude of a servant, as Jesus gave the example to
the disciples even as he was to endure death and
horrible punishments."

Editor. Mish, Frederick. Merriam Webster Dictionary, 11th ed.
Merriam Webster, Inc.: Springfield, Mass., 2004, p. 1369.

> "Unity: the quality or state of not being multiple ...
> oneness ... a condition of harmony, accord. Unite:
> to act in concert. Union: a uniting in marriage."

Editor. http://www.mtjuliet.org/sermons/archives/00wl43.html
"Early Church History of the Church of Christ," Mt. Juliet
Church of Christ, Vol. 18, No. 6, June 2013, p. 7.

> "The Bible vividly portrays the nature of the
> church in the various descriptive titles. These
> show its relationship to Christ and to the world,
> as well as the relationship of members one to
> another ... as a body, it is united. No member is
> unnecessary, each cares for the other, and all are
> joined to the Head (I Cor. 12).

Esler, Philip F. Conflict and Identity in Romans. Fortress Press:
Minneapolis, 2003, p. 361.

> "To solidify his message of the oneness of God
> and the unity of the Christian movement Paul
> develops the image of Abraham as a prototype of
> the new identity in chapter 4 of Romans."

Fee, Gordon. How to Read the Bible for All Its Worth. Zondervan
Publishing House: Grand Rapids, Michigan, 1982, p. 88.

> "By and large, most sectors of evangelical
> Protestantism have "restoration movement"
> mentality. We regularly look back to the church

and Christian experience in the first century either as the norm to be restored or the ideal to be approximated."

Fee, Gordon. How to Read the Bible for All Its Worth (updated). Zondervan Publishing House: Grand Rapids, Michigan, 2002, p. 351.

"Note that the narrative and prayer are now followed by imperative words of exhortation. This is how Paul addresses his third major concern—that the Ephesian believers maintain 'the unity of the Spirit' noted in Eph. 2: 11-22. Thus the exhortation to 'be filled with the Spirit' (Eph. 5:18) for worship also serves as a hinge between relationships in general and within households in particular, where worship would take place."

Fee, Gordon. Paul, the Spirit, and the People of God. Hendrickson Publications, Inc.: Peabody, Massachusetts, 1996, p. 71.

"Paul argues first that the many of them (Jew, Gentile, slave, free) are one body because of their common lavish experience of Spirit (I Cor. 12) ... likewise, in Philippi, where some bickering and posturing were going on that could lead to disunity, Paul urges his readers, especially in light of their struggle against pagan opponents, to 'stand firm in one Spirit' (Phil. 1:27) ... unity in the body means that believers 'walk by the Spirit' so as not to eat and devour one another (Gal. 3) ... it also requires heterogeneous people to submit their diversity to the unifying work of the Spirit ...

such churches cannot maintain the unity of the Spirit that Paul taught in Ephesians 2 and 4 and I Corinthians 12."

Fee, Gordon. New Testament Exegesis. Westminster/John Knox Press (revised): Louisville, Kentucky, 1993, p. 34.

"(regarding exegesis of N.T. writings) Read the entire document through in English in one sitting … there is no substitute for this step. You never start exegeting a book at chapter 1, verse 1. The first step always is to read the entire document through before analyzing any of its parts, and you gain such a sense by reading it through."

Frease, James. "The Doctrines of the Christian Faith: What Do You Believe?" World Changers Bible Institute: Mt. Juliet, Tennessee, 2013, p. 6.

"There is a difference between union and unity. Certainly there are core doctrines and belief that are the basis of being a Christian believer. That is founded on what one must do to be a true believer … become a born-again believer. There are other doctrines that are core and essential to basic Christian believers … Jesus was the savior for all who want eternal life as a gift by God's grace … one must be obedient to the commandments of Jesus to function as a part of the church or Body of Christ. But when one gets into playing with snakes, or keeping people from Christ because a man wears earrings or the lady has too short a haircut, this is the area of unity across the board that reflects the demands of the Pharisees of the Old Covenant. People have preferences that are fringe issues, not foundational to being a true believer, or in union."

Galli, Mark. Christianity Today, "Whatever Happened to Grace?", Oct. 2013, p. 23-24.

"But in the beginning is grace. In the middle is grace. In the end, 'all manner of thing shall be well' (Julian of Norwich) because of grace. What I'm hearing time and again, in every corner of the church I visit, is not the soaring message of grace, but a dull message of works—that I have a certain feeling, or perspire in effort before I can be assured of God's radical acceptance and my future salvation."

George, Bob. Classic Christianity. Harvest House Publishers: Eugene, Oregon, 1989, p. 69.

"After many years spent talking with people of all denominations from every part of the country, I picture the average Christian's understanding to be much as mine was: like a person with a big box of jigsaw puzzle pieces, each piece representing a Bible verse, a sermon illustration, or a doctrine they have been taught. If you have been a Christian very long at all, you have probably accumulated quite a collection! Especially in twentieth-century America, which I believe has received more Christian education than any group in the last 2000 years. All those puzzle pieces … but we don't know how to put them together!"

Furlong, Gary T. The Conflict Resolution Toolbox. John Wiley & Sons: Canada, Ltd., 2005, p. 137.

"How Attributions Form: Motives and intentions cannot be seen, they can only be inferred from our interpretation of the other party's behavior. Attributions, therefore, are fundamentally perceptions, not reality. Perceptions are influenced mostly by two factors: information and preconceptions … Still, attributions can be changed. As practitioners, we can help to influence parties' attributions by working with or challenging the two elements that form attributions, namely, information and preconceptions."

Gladner, Paul. Christianity Today: NY Times author, p. 53.

"People use the Bible to support their pre-determined view."

Graham, Franklin. Decision. "A National Wake-up Call," Billy Graham Evangelistic Association: Charlotte, North Carolina, Nov. 2013, p. 40.

"In the past five decades, our nation seems to have done everything it can to marginalize the role of faith and religion in our society. The rise of pluralism and tolerance has sought to dilute the influence of Christianity."

Grimsley, Shawn. http://education-portal.com/academy "Unity of Command in Management: Principle, Definition and Quiz," July 2014, p. 1 of 2.

> "The principle of unity of command is applied throughout the world today in organizations ranging from military, government bureaucracies and companies, from small business all the way up to multinational corporations ... unity of command provides that an employee is responsible to only one supervisor, who in turn is responsible to only one supervisor, and so on up the organizational hierarchy. This is true even if the top of the organization is led by a group of people."

Haley, John W. Alleged Discrepancies of the Bible. Baker Book House: Grand Rapids, Michigan, 1977, p. 60.

> "I John 5:7 is a spurious passage. It is found in no Greek manuscript before the Fifteenth or sixteenth century, and in no early version. It is rejected by Alford, Abbot, Bleek ... and most modern critics."

Harrelson, Walter J. The New Interpreter's Study Bible. Abington Press: Nashville, TN, 2003, p. 2094.

> "These verses (Eph. 4: 1-16) explain why the church is unified and what behaviors Make for unity ... (4: 4-6) lists the seven (perfect number) reasons for church unity."

Horner, Noel. United Church of God. "Heaven or Hell: What Does the Bible Really Teach?", 2009, p. 6.

> "Traditional beliefs about heaven and hell are based on an underlying teaching—that Everyone has an immortal soul that must go somewhere when physical life ends. This belief isn't unique to traditional Christianity, 'All religions affirm that there is an aspect of the human person that lives on after the physical life has ended ... in other words, in general, some kind of immortal essence, a spirit that lives on separately after the physical body dies. Most professing Christians call this the immortal soul."

Hooser, Don. (personal correspondence department). United Church of God: Cincinnati, Ohio, March, 2014, p. 1 of 2.

> "(Regarding a letter sent to the UCOG for a statement on church unity, the response) People often get what they ask for. You asked to understand the teachings of some church leaders. Satan answered by hitting you with his counterfeit spirituality."

Howard, Jeremy Royal. (editor) Holman Christian Standard Bible. Holman Bible Publishers: Nashville, Tennessee, 2010, p. 2033, 1602.

> "Believers have the responsibility to keep unity in the body of Christ. The seven 'ones' enumerated in these verses constitute the foundation on which the Trinitarian God creates a oneness in the

church. Paul's plan can be seen from the vantage point of the work of the one Spirit, creating one body, the one Lord Jesus Christ creating one hope, faith, and baptism, and the one God the Father bringing about one people of God … One God and Father of all reminds believers that God's oneness defines the church's oneness."

"It seems fitting that the first book of the New Testament, the Gospel of Matthew— begins with these words: 'the historical record of Jesus.' This Gospel was written from a strong Jewish perspective to show that Jesus truly is the Messiah promised in the Old Testament."

Hunter, Samuel Micah. The American Journal of Biblical Theology. "The Unity of the Church and the Kiss as its Biblical Expression," Dec. 2010, p. 6, 10.

"At the suggestion that the kiss is appropriate for use in the modern American church, I expect to encounter a fair degree of resistance. I believe that the major contribution to this resistance is a concern regarding what kind of kiss is being suggested. … I contend that a proper understanding of Christian unity necessitates a true identification of believers as family."

Inglis, James. A Topical Dictionary of Bible Texts. Baker Book House: Grand Rapids, Michigan, 1968, p. 104-105.

"(A listing of 12 references within the N.T. describing Church Unity) John 10:16; John 17:11;

Rom. 12:4; I Cor. 10:17,12:5; Gal. 3:26; Eph. 1:10, 2:15, 3:6, 4:4, 4:16; Col. 3:11."

Irons, Lee, PhD. "The Framework Interpretation of the Days of Creation," Christian Research Institute: Charlotte, NC, 2003, p. 1 of 4.

"The issue of literal interpretation of portions of scripture over the possible use of a figurative one, as in a metaphor or illustrative parable or other form of poetic effort to convey a larger concept or meaning is illustrated in this article to attest that the first chapter of Genesis can and must be seen as non-literal, as Moses is suggested to have a larger purpose in the way of the days of Creation are presented. This is an example of how issues of interpretation beyond simple word of phrase meanings can lead to separation of groups of Christian believers."

Jamieson, Robert. Commentary on the Whole Bible. Regency Reference Library, Zondervan Publishing House: Grand Rapids, Michigan, 1961, p. 1289.

"The 'true' body of Christ (all believers of every age) is already 'one,' as joined to the one Head. But its unity is as yet not visible; even as the Head is not visible; but it shall appear when He shall appear (Jn. 17:21-23, Col. 3:4)."

Jeremiah, David. Invasion of Other Gods. Word Publishing: Dallas, TX, 1995, p. 191.

> "Jesus said, 'Heaven and earth will pass away, but my words will by no means pass Away. But of that day and hour no one knows ... only the Father ... Jesus also said There would be a generation which would see all the signs unfold that would signal His soon return. One evidence would be a one-world government joined with a unified religious system. Both on are the horizon today."

Kaleem, Jaweed. www.huffingtonpost.com "U.S. Roman Catholic Church and Protestant Denominations Agree to Recognize Each Other's Baptisms," July 2014, p. 1 of 5.

> "Currently, the Protestant churches recognize Roman Catholic baptisms, but the Catholic church does not always recognize theirs. The mutual agreement on baptisms, a key sacrament in the churches, has been discussed between denominational leadership for seven years and hinges in part on invoking trinity of the 'Father, Son and Holy Spirit' during the baptism."

Kalin, Ibrahim. www.resetdoc.org/story. "Religion, Unity and Diversity," Feb. 2014, p. 1 of 7.

> "The terms unity, integration and diversity have multiple layers of meaning in the Religious context ... when understood properly, unity does not mean uniformity ... diversity does not mean disorder ... a broader understanding of these

terms will help and lead us to a more critical assessment of the Enlightenment and Western modernity ... conceptually, our minds conceive things not as discrete and disconnected items but as an interconnected unity ... it is the unity between heaven and earth that generates order, proportion, balance and harmony in the world."

Klein, William W. Introduction to Biblical Interpretation. Word Publishing: Dallas, TX, 1993, p. 168.

"(Content of the Entire Bible) This final element is more controversial and more difficult to control. As we presupposed, the Bible possesses a unity in its parts in spite of its diversity of human authors. Scripture's divine inspiration gives continuity of thought to books written over a 1500 year period ... Because of this unity, the entire Bible provides a literacy context for all passages in it. But here comes the controversy and the difficulty. How do we allow individual authors their unique perspectives—the Bible's diversity—and yet affirm the Bible's unity?"

Kouzes, James M. The Leadership Challenge. Jossey-Bass Publishers: San Francisco, CA, 1990, p. 10.

"To enlist people in a vision, a leader must 'know your followers and speak their language,' according to the organization development manager at McKesson. People must believe that you understand their needs and have their interests at heart. Only through an intimate knowledge of their dreams, their hopes, their aspirations, their visions, their values is the leader able to enlist their support.

LaBissoniere, John. The Good News. "What Do You Believe and Why?" Nov-Dec 2013, p. 28-29.

> "How do you know if what you believe is really true? Is it possible you have been influenced to believe things that are wrong? How does it happen ... it's because their views have been formed as a result of tradition, hearsay or information not based on fact or properly researched. (Conventional beliefs regarding the Sabbath and how long Jesus was in the grave before his resurrection are listed as ideas not supported by what the New Testament actually states ... editor)."

Leavy, Jane. The Last Boy, Mickey Mantle. HarperCollins Publishers: New York, 2010, p. 204.

> "(After having lost the final game of the world series to the Pirates ... his wife Merlyn told a crying Mickey as they flew home), 'Mickey, its only a game.'"

Luo, Michael. Christianity Today. "All the Faith That's Fit to Print," Dec. 2013, p. 53.

> "(When asked about the death of a famous pastor's son ... regarding guns, this New York Times writer stated) 'In a good faith attempt to answer your question, it seems to me that this is

one of those issues in which many people simply take the Bible and apply it in a way that fits their existing viewpoint.'"

MacDonald, William. Believer's Bible Commentary. Thomas Nelson Publishers: Nashville, TN, 1995, p. 1932-1933.

"Our exalted standing in Christ calls for corresponding godly conduct ... as pointed out previously, these closing chapters of Ephesians, 4-6, teach that 'we must cultivate unity in the church, purity in our personal lives, harmony in our homes, and stability in our combat with the powers of evil ... to keep the unity of the Spirit means to live at peace with one another. They should give diligence to keep the unity of the Spirit. The Holy Spirit has made all true believers one in Christ; the Body is indwelt by the one Spirit ... denominations, sects, and parties hinder the outworking of this truth. All such man-made divisions will be swept away when the Savior returns."

MacPhail, Bryan. www.reformedtheology.ca/ephesians4a.htm MacPhail's Manuscripts, "A Unified Church," Oct. 2013, p. 1 of 3.

"What I hope to demonstrate in this sermon from Scriptures, is the nature of the unity we are called to ... it is called to a unity that mirrors the unity of the Trinity. As Jesus stated in Jn. 17, 'that they (the Church) may be one, as (He and the Father) are one.' Through humility, patience, forbearance and love, we are not asking the church to be same as everyone else. Rather, it is becoming like Jesus Christ ... Paul referred to growing in the faith as a race, so it is imperative that we guard the 'one faith' by holding to common beliefs and striving to a common goal. Paul challenges each of us to pull toward the goal in unison."

Malphurs, Aubrey. Developing a Vision for Ministry in the 21st Century. Baker Books: Grand Rapids, Michigan, 2004, p. 20.

"An institutional vision is one of the critical components of unity in ministry. The Vision affects a least two areas of organizational unity ... the first area of unity is in the recruitment of ministry personnel. They can decide in advance if their personal vision closely matches the organization's direction ... the second area is in the retention of ministry personnel ... New Testament ministry is team ministry (Acts 11: 22-30, etc.), who make significant but different contributions from their gifts and varied personalities ... vision is the leaders key to holding the team together."

Martin, Walter. The Kingdom of the Cults (revised). Bethany House Publishers: Minneapolis, Minnesota, 1997, p. 333.

"The New Age movement is not easily defined. It has no specific founder, primary leader, central headquarters, organizational structure, or definitive statement of beliefs. Nor does it meet in any one place or at any one particular time. It is not even limited to one single group. As a result, the New Age movement is described in a variety of different ways … they hold many common beliefs, but often hold numerous distinctive doctrines … even disagreeing with each other on significant issues … they do not fit the classic definition of a cult."

Maxwell, John C. The 21 Most Powerful Minutes in a Leader's Day. Thomas Nelson Publishers: Nashville, TN, 2000, p. 73, 189.

"We are not here to compete with each other, but to complete each other … Theodore Roosevelt said, 'the best executive is one who has the sense enough to pick good men to do what he wants done, and the self-restraint enough to keep from meddling with them while they do it.'"

McReynolds, Paul R. Work Study Greek-English New Testament. Tydale House Publishers: Wheaton, Illinois, 1999, p. 401.

"(United Bible Societies: 3rd Edition) John 17:11 … 'And no longer I am in the world, and themselves in the world are, and I to you come. Father holy, keep them in the name of you that you have given me, that they might be one just as we.'"

Metzger, Paul Louis. Christianity Today, Why Unity is So Hard, Nov. 2013, p. 71

"(A review of a book by Christena Cleveland … Disunity in Christ) Christians value Jesus' prayer that they—his followers—may be as one (Jn. 17).

But valuing Christian unity is not the same as realizing it ... individual personalities, faults, and sins are not the only factors. Group dynamics also make a difference.

'Sometimes ... we are affected in hidden ways by those around us ... Perfect love castes out all fear needs to be attended to in I Jn. 4, as ultimately each group advocates strict positions, yet we are to love each other, and encourage the others to recognize the need to review their stand in the light of God's Word ... truth."

Mead, Frank S. Handbook of Denominations in the United States. Abington Press: Nashville, Tennessee, 1988, p. 175-176.

"(Unity of the Brethren) Known until 1962 as the Evangelical Unity of the Czech-Moravian Brethren in North America, this body originated among immigrants Arriving in Texas in the late nineteenth century ... their present name originated in the year 1457."

Miller, Stephen M. The Complete Guide to the Bible. Barbour Publishing, Inc.: Uhrichsville, Ohio, 2007, p. 411.

"Paul calls for unity in the churches, but not unity at all costs (Eph. 4) ... for he warns in Acts 20:30, "some men from your own group will rise up and distort the truth in order to draw a following ... he goes on in Ephesians 4 to confront these people, but in peace, for there is one Lord, faith, baptism, God and Father."

Montgomery, John Warwick. Faith Founded on Fact. Trinity Press: Newburgh, Indiana, 2002, p. 96-97, 132-133.

> "The reader has undoubtedly been impressed (as has the writer) with the similarity Between many of Muhammad Ali's arguments for Islam and the defenses for the Christian faith presented by not a few Christian theologians … his main apologetic is in the area of subjectively empirical argument … the means adopted are an appeal to the reasoning faculty, an appeal to the heart of man …"

> "We are told that, as those who go by Luther's name, we should be the last to approach Christianity apologetically … as the young Luther had little interest in 'natural theology—in the knowledge of God or of divine truth that can be attained by the sinner in his unregenerate state— and how ended up taking an existential position on the issue. Thus the arguments continue for support of the belief in natural theology."

No Author listed. www.opc.org/relations/unity Orthodox Presbyterian Church. "Biblical Principles of the Unity of the Church, Nov. 2013, p. 1-9.

> "The church is the covenant people of God in all ages and among all nations … in the New Testament this teaching of the unity of the people of God is sustained … the unity of the church is attained unto by growing in spiritual maturity (Eph. 4). As we take account of the diversity

that exists between denominations arising from differences of ethnic identity, cultural background, and historical circumstance the most conclusive evidence derived from Scripture is required to support the position that the obliteration of denominational separateness is an obligation resting upon these church of Christ ... though the diversity which manifests itself in differentiating historical development might appear to make ecclesiastical union inadvisable or even perilous in certain cases, yet the biblical evidence in support of union is so plain that any argument to the contrary, however plausible, must be false."

Palmer, John L. (editor). The Reagan Record: An Urban Institute Study. Ballinger Publishing Company: Cambridge, Massachusetts, 1984, p. 222

"Reagan's alternative vision of federalism can be summarized in three phrases: 'separation of powers,' 'devolution of responsibilities to governments that are closer to the people,' and 'less spending by all levels of government ... it is now argued that lines of accountability have been blurred by this overlapping of authority across the three distinct powers of the federal government."

Parshall, Craig. Israel My Glory. "A More Perfect Union: The Biblical Bottom Line," November 2013, p. 13.

"Biblical fidelity and the belief in the authenticity and plenary inspiration of Scripture is becoming increasingly important for the church, particularly as America continues its downward slide from being irritably impatient to condemning those who take the Bible seriously. As things progress, the church will be tempted to avoid clearly teaching the Word."

Parshall, Craig. Israel My Glory. "Why We Believe," January 2014, p. 13.

"...this should not come as a surprise, as God's Word tells us the same thing: The Spirit Himself bears witness with our spirit that we are the children of God (Rom. 8:16). Why do we believe? Because God's truth is factual, intellectually coherent, and consistent with real life. And when we trust in His Son, God imprints it indelibly on our hearts."

Paul, The Apostle. "Ephesians 4: 1-3, 11-13," The New Testament, NASV: Hendrickson Publishers: Peabody, MA, 1995, p. 908-909.

"Therefore I, as a prisoner of the Lord, implore you to walk in a manner worthy of calling with which you have been called, with all humility and gentleness, with patience, showing tolerance for one another in love, being diligent to preserve the unity of the spirit in the bond of peace." "And He gave some as apostles, and some as prophets, and some as evangelists, and some as pastors, and teachers for the equipping of the saints for the work of service, to the building up of the body of Christ; until we all attain to the unity of the faith, and of the knowledge of the Son of God, to a mature man, to the measure of the stature which belongs to the fullness of Christ."

Rendle, Gilbert. Leading Change in the Congregation. An Alban Institute Publication: Cokesbury, Pennsylvania, 1998, p. 52-53.

"(General Systems Theory) For several centuries our culture, with its Western European beginnings, has looked at the structure of experience using a mechanistic worldview. According to this view, the world is much like a machine made of component parts all working together in synchronized fashion to some purposeful end. To understand that world and one's place and purpose in it, break the larger machine into its component parts and seek to understand the individual parts and how they work together … there are other ways, different languages, and less mechanistic ideas that we can use to help us to understand and to respond to our congregations more appropriately. Systems theory provides a helpful, more organic language and ideas that give rise to more appropriate responses, responses beyond solving problems and seeking control … focusing on on nourishing and nurturing the system, not just fixing it."

Richards, Larry. Every Teaching of Jesus in the Bible. Thomas Nelson Publishers: Nashville, Tennessee, 2001, p. 205-206.

"Prayer that all believers might be one (Jn. 17: 20-23). This is undoubtedly the most misunderstood element of Jesus' prayer. Many people have viewed it as a call to organizational unity. Many sermons have been preached and many well-intentioned movements have been launched based on a misinterpretation of these verses ... the unity of which Jesus spoke is organic. It is unity which believers can have with the Lord, not with one another. This oneness is clearly defined in the text: 'as you, Father, are in Me, and I in you' ... 'that they also may be one in Us' ... 'I in them, and You in Me.'"

Rogers, Ronnie W. Undermining the Gospel: The Case for Church Discipline. Pleasant Word: Enumclaw, Washington, 2004, p. 18.

"The lack of church discipline contributes to subverting the gospel in three crucial ways. First, it allows those who are carnal, immoral, divisive, doctrinally deviate, and /or unregenerate to remain in our churches, and thereby, corrupt the purpose, fellowship and credibility of the church ... undermines the gospel by supporting our culture's growing contempt for discipline ... and when the pastor leads in the easy areas of church obligations and services and ignores the more difficult it sets the church congregation up for less than full implementation of God's divine intervention in the work of the Body of Christ."

Ryrie, Charles Caldwell. The Ryrie Study Bible: New American Standard Bible, The Lockman Foundation: Chicago, Illinois, 2010, p. 1426.

"(I Cor. 12: 12-31) Here Paul describes the relationship of gifted believers to each other, using the analogy of the human body. The Spirit has formed a spiritual organic unity of the many dissimilar members of the Body of Christ. The constitutions both of the human body and the Body of Christ demand that all members (even those that seem unimportant) function in harmony."

Sande, Ken. The Peacemaker Church Implementation Manual. www.peacemaker.net Peacemaker Ministries: Billings, Montana, 2005, p. 185.

"Unity: we usually resolve disagreements over vision and goals in a constructive manner. The spirit of harmony and sincere love in our church allows us to work toward our goals effectively. Our leaders seek true unity (sincere agreement) rather than an imposed uniformity. The power of the gospel is revealed in our church by a growing unity, harmony, and stability in marriages, leadership, and membership. Peacemaking has helped people resolve conflicts that otherwise might have caused them to leave our church. People seldom leave our church because of personal conflicts."

Sison, Matites N. "Christian Unity: What Does God Require of Us?" Anglican Journal. October 2013.

> "Week of Prayer for Christian Unity (this year from Jan. 18-25, 2013) is celebrated by over two billion Christians world-wide ... this year's theme is 'What does God require of us? (Micah 6: 6-8) 'What the Lord does require of you, but to do justice, to love kindness, and work humbly with your God.'" " ...a sampling of WofPforCU celebrations across Canada ... bishop gave lecture on 'How Communion Changes Ecumenism.'" " ...a collaboration service will be conducted by Catholic, Baptist, United Church of Canada, Presbyterian and Evangelical Lutheran pastors."

Stauffer, Clay. Woodmont Christian Church, Nashville, TN. The Tennessean, "Christianity's Core Message has been Watered Down," Nov 2013, Local News, p. 3b.

> "So before we get too wrapped up with doctrine, biblical liberalism, worship styles, social issues, and church shopping, we should ask ourselves, 'How are we doing when it comes to following these two commandments?' I grew up as a preacher's kid hearing my father talk about the cross. The vertical bar represents our relationship to God (worship, prayer, Bible study, stewardship, etc.). The horizontal bar represents our relationship to others (mission, service, outreach, kindness). Without both bars, we don't have the cross. Without both aspects of the faith, Christianity is incomplete. Mark 12 gives the answer to the core

of Christian faith. Jesus told the Jewish leader that the two commandments of loving God with all one's life and likewise, one's neighbor as oneself is the basic tenet of Christianity."

Smietana, Bob. The Tennessean Newspaper. "Churches Walk Fine Line on Immigration Issue," 2013, Local News Section.

"Not all Baptists agree with the resolution [calls for immigration reform but asks all congregations to assist undocumented aliens in need]."

Strauch, Alexander. Biblical Eldership: Urgent Call to Restore Biblical Church Eldership. Lewis and Roth Publishers: Colorado Springs, Colorado, 1995, p. 96.

"Conflict among elders is a serious, all-to-common problem. It is appalling how little regard some Christians leaders have for the sacredness of the unity of the body of Christ, and how quickly they will divide the body in order to gain their own way. In the end they may get their own way, but it is not God's way ... The Christian solution is to humble oneself, love as Christ loved, wash one another's feet, repent, submit, pray, turn from pride, shun impatience, and honor and love one another."

Slick, Matt. Christian Apologetics and Research Ministry, "The Need for Unity in the Church," http://carm.org/need-unity-church Oct. 2013, p. 1 of 2.

"What is it that unites us? Primarily it is the saving work of Christ that unites us. Secondarily, it is the essential doctrines that define orthodoxy. We have, as a common heritage, the blood of Christ that has been shed for the forgiveness of our sins … furthermore, we have the body of Scriptures which tell us the essentials of the faith … it is the essential doctrines that we must know to unite us."

Strecker, Georg. Theology of the New Testament. Westminster John Knox Press: Louisville, Kentucky, 2000, p. 191.

"There was no clearly defined office of leadership in the Pauline congregations. The reality of the body of Christ was the overarching concept, and the unity and unanimity of the church that had within it the functions of community leadership without needing to make claims to hierarchical office, for the fundamental operative principle was: church leadership is a charisma, a gift of the Spirit. No one has the right to set this or that gift absolutely above the others in which the reality of the Spirit's presence in the congregation was experienced."

Strobel, Lee. The Case for the Real Jesus. Zondervan: Grand Rapids, Michigan, 2007, p. 71, 98.

"You can't interpret the text without certain biases, but we should challenge our biases as much as possible."

"It's disturbing that when it comes to the Christian faith, people don't really want—or know how—to investigate the evidence ... Christians are not being led into proper historical research by their pastors."

Tenney, Merrill C. The New Testament Survey. Wm. B. Eerdman's Publishing Co. Intervarsity Press: Grand Rapids, Michigan, 1985, p. 321.

"Ephesians is a specimen of his 'Bible Conference' technique. Much of its material can be duplicated in his other epistles, and there is little theology or ethics in Ephesians that cannot be found in essence elsewhere. The total complex, however is integrated into a new picture of the church as a single functioning body, created out of Jew and Gentile, equipped with standards of its own, and engaged in a spiritual conflict. It's goal is 'unity of the faith ... the knowledge of the Son of God ... the increase of the stature of the fullness of Christ (Eph. 4:13).'"

Towns, Elmer. Eleven Innovations in the Local Church. Regal Books: Ventura, California, 2007, p. 26-27.

"In his book, 'Organic Church,' Cole observes that 'the world is interested in Jesus; it is His wife (the Church is the bride of Christ) that they do not want to spend time with.' Lamenting that 'the local church no longer has the influence to change the world,' he observes, 'Something is wrong with the way we are doing church here.' His assessment is that too many established, facility-based churches have 'lost the plot' along the way. 'Attendance on Sundays does not transform lives; Jesus with their hearts is what changes people.' Cole is not alone. In "Revolution" evangelical researcher George Barna claims that in the year 2000, most of the nation's organized religious activity took place at or through local churches. Today, according to Barna, the action is increasingly shifting to forms of religious commitment that lack any connection to a local church ... these are attending a house church in the local community."

Tozer, A. W. The Pursuit of God. Christian Publications, Inc.: Camp Hill, Pennsylvania, 1982, p. 101.

"Much of our difficulty as seeking Christians stems from our unwillingness to take God as He is and adjust our lives accordingly. We insist upon trying to modify Him and to bring Him nearer to our own image."

Tyson, Joseph B. A Study of Early Christianity. The Macmillan Company: New York, 1973, p. 341.

"A genuinely biographical interest in Jesus is a peculiarly modern one. Prior to the middle of the eighteenth century, the Christian either accepted the four canonical Gospels as strictly accurate historical records or else neglected history altogether ... One of the chief problems has been the perspective of the modern scholar. Although this is a major problem in any historical writing, the study of the life of Jesus has been particularly plagued by it ... this being a number of anachronisms in biographies of

Jesus … usually in inoffensive ways, [editor: but nevertheless speculations or subjective extensions of implications in the gospel texts."

Vine, W. E. An Expository Dictionary of Biblical Words. Thomas Nelson Publishers: Nashville, Tennessee, 1984, p. 1183.

"HENOTES (evorns..Gk), from *hen*, the neuter of *heis*, **one**, is used in Eph. 4:3,13."

Washington, Raleigh. Break Down the Walls: Experiencing Biblical Reconciliation and Unity in the Body of Christ. Moody Press: Chicago, Illinois, 1997, p. 60-61.

"We are all called to a ministry of reconciliation, and we're all commanded to be reconciled with our brothers across racial, cultural, and denominational barriers … Where love and unity exist the body, God is being honored … Satan has the goal of keeping us divided. Christ has a goal for us to love one another and be united."

Watts, Craig M. "Church Unity and the Necessity of Non-Violence," Journal of Ecumenical Studies, Vol. 39, No. 3-4, Sum-Fall 2002.

"A lack of unity discredits the witness and work of the church for the world. This truth has long been emphasized by those concerned for the oneness of the church … the church's sanction of war and the participation of its members, in various forms of violence is the most glaring and harmful expression of disunity." [He cites the

World Council of Churches constitution for the purpose of gaining unity through the common life in Christ.] [First Assembly of World Council of Churches proclaimed, 'We are one in proclaiming to all (that war) is contrary to the will of God.']

Welch, Robert H. Church Administration: Creating Efficiency for Effective Ministry. Broadman and Holman Publishers: Nashville, Tennessee, 2005, p. 42-44.

"...we will discuss four dysfunctional (leadership) styles that are prevalent in the Church today ... the Showman: has an inflated view of their leadership position and Ability ... the Doubting Thomas: has not developed the ability to rely upon those they lead ... The Monk: this is an individualist, doing his role with no interaction with others in the congregation ... The Control Freak: assures that the organization functions exactly as this leader dictates."

White, J. E. The Gospel Primer. Southern Publishing Association: Nashville, Tennessee, 1901, p. 113.

"In this valley was the city of Sychar, and outside the gates of the city was a well, called the well of Jacob. Jesus, being weary and footsore, sat down by the well to rest ... as he sat by the well, a woman of Samaria came to draw water ... she ignored Jesus as he was a Jew ... but Jesus asked for a drink ... she asked why he spoke to her, since they (Jews and Samaritans) did not communicate at all. [Jesus' response was one of the first indications of the fact that the gospel was not just for the Jews, but for the whole world.] He said, "If you knew the gift of God, and who it is that says to you, 'Give me drink,' you would have asked of him, and he would have given you living water.'"

Wood, George O. The Evangel (Assemblies of God), "Servant Leader," Springfield, Missouri, June 2012, p. 30.

"Jesus stated in Mk. 10:43-45: ' … whoever wants to become great among you must be your servant, and whoever wants to be first must be a slave to all' … if you long for greatness and a lead position, then Jesus has advice … it is working your way to the bottom to support everyone else … sadly the church has not always listened to Him. I've seen too many instances in the local church and in national bodies of believers where selfish ambition, cloaked in 'spirituality,' flatly ignores Jesus' teaching … they always put their own interests ahead of the unity of the Body."

Yancey, Philip. Meet the Bible. Zondervan Press: Grand Rapids, Michigan, 2000, p. 274.

"Corrie ten Boom tells of an ultimate test of her willingness to let God love Through her a person she had every reason to hate. [summary: after speaking to a crowd in 1947, she noticed a face she could not forget … one of the Nazi guards who oversaw the concentration camp in which she was jailed along with a sister who died there … as he left he stopped to shake her hand tell

# APPENDIX A

## Statements from Local Pastors in the Nashville, Tennessee Area

The basic question presented to the pastor or other ordained individual or long-term leader of a particular congregation: When the Bible teaches or speaks to the topic of "Unity in the Church," what exactly does that mean?

**Church of Christ**: This individual was rather hesitant to answer ... as he took a while and asked me to repeat the question. (Note: I realized that it would be important for any further interviews to be more introductory and explain the intent of my question on this topic of unity more completely.) Upon repeating the question, he told me that it was important for me to realize that each of the Church of Christ congregations is autonomous ... they do not belong to a national oversight association ... all leadership develops within the local congregation. So he pointed to the local congregation as the place of unity. If one attends, one must agree with the local teachings. One of them is that instruments are not used to accompany congregational singing. Unity is a matter of learning and working to comply with the teachings of the local Church of Christ. Their determination is to promote unity by going back to "just the Bible" in determining what to believe and how to practice their Christian life.

**Southern Baptist:** The pastor of a local congregation was quite open about the issues of the subject of unity in the Body of Christ. One of the things he wanted to point out was the fact that in his mind there is a distinct difference between unity and uniformity. His point was that too often sincere and genuine Christians are after everyone in the Body of Christ wearing the same uniform, using the same translation of the Bible and singing exactly the same songs. Of course they would have to have the exact same said to them as they were being baptized, and only being immersed in a specially made casing for baptizing behind the church choir loft. His point was clear to the fact that unity is in Christ and our relationship with Him, not how alike we are in the secondary issues.

**Roman Catholic:** Approaching this facility was not as easy as most of the others, as the access to the local priest who was responsible for the entire local facility involved coming up through quite a series of stairs, doors and screening clerical staff. That experience, set me up to expect quite an opportunity to hear from the representatives from the largest Christian institution in our world today. Upon entering the actual office, the priest was apparently quite involved in various preparatory matters and found my entering his area a bit intrusive. I quickly introduced myself and my intent. He looked at me for a short moment and abruptly told me that I should contact or read what the Pope has said. So for the leaders of the Roman Catholic dioceses their teaching on the topic of unity in the Body of Christ is simply a matter of hearing what the Pope says and accepting his jurisdiction over the matter.

**Evangelical Luthern:** This pastor was alone and attending to the notes of his next Sunday sermon. He is a pastor of a small congregation, yet they support a food bank for the local area to assist some families enduring financial difficulties. His response to question about church unity was a hard one for him to answer, as he was clearly committed to his job and yet he was quite supportive of the need for the Christians of this world to join in their cooperative effort to reach them with the Gospel message. Although he did not say it directly, his overall comments showed a sincere commitment to being a part of joining the groups of Christians into a cooperative effort to be a Christian team to reach the world for Christ's Gospel message. He pointed out that too often the differences developed out of good distances between groups of people geographically, so over time the local practices developed and became the tradition of how church services and outreaches were conducted. He did add that the outside culture of the people of America has had a significant impact on the necessity for each Christian group to take serious inventory of what they are doing to reach the world for Christ … what actual practices and local traditions are biblically sound and critical to help non-Christians come to a saving knowledge of Jesus.

**"Non-denominational" (cross-denominational) Church Pastors:** Two local pastors were interviewed, each representing separate unrelated church groups. The pastor of the largest congregation was also adamant about the difference between unity and uniformity. He insisted on making the point that the core message of the gospel did not change, but how one presents it to the public (non-believers) is the essential area of the necessity for change to accommodate the cultural and societal changes. He was not a electronic or technical expert, but depended on those volunteers in his congregation to develop a multiple series of applications to enhance the services, sermons and musical efforts presented in the weekend and mid-week services.

The second pastor of the "cross-denominational" local congregation was also quite committed to using "updated" methods to reach out to the local community to present the message of the gospel. He believed that the people attending and beginning to join their group were seeing that the church they had attended was not making the necessary up dates to how the church served the congregation, so because they wanted their children to also stay interested they changed and began attending the newer cross-denominational church group.

**Presbyterian (the version of it formed in the Nashville area ... Cumberland Presbyterian):** This represents interviews combined across three of these congregations and in one case a long-time member of one of them. It seemed to present a very similar type of Christian group as found at the Southern Baptist groups. Apparently the organizational hierarchy of the Presbyterian groups are much more structured than the Southern Baptist, as pointed out by one of the pastors being interviewed. He informed me that the Southern Baptist still maintain a local governing board that determines the choices of pastor, and other leaders. In the Presbyterian group, the determination of pastor is a matter of selection by higher ups within the national, regional association. Unity is promoted by cooperating within the national and regional orders. This creates a commonality in all local groups/congregations.

# APPENDIX B

# Keys to Unity on a Personal Level

1. The individual member must be a Christian … Born Again by the Spirit of God
2. The individual member must be led by the Spirit of God, showing the fruits of the Spirit: love, joy, peace, patience, kindness, goodness, faithfulness, gentleness and self-control.
3. The individual member must be a servant and/or a servant leader … the greatest among you (the Church or Body of Christ) is your servant.
4. The individual member must be convicted to work for unity … make it a high priority in all actions taken and decisions made.
5. The individual member, as a part of the Body of Christ, as a brother or sister to other members, must recognize Satan's commitment to undermine any unity within the church.
6. The group of Christians, whether denomination, local congregation, or small community Bible study group, or charitable associations, must have guidance through servant leadership.
7. Culture, race, and ethnicity bear heavily on unity by simple unintentional differences … As mortals in this world we immediately sense "differences" and perceive them first of all as strange, shocking, unusual, not like my understanding,

and any number of screenings we naturally tend to do, when confronted with that which we are unaccustomed to deal with. We often become defensive and assume that the difference must not be right ... therefore, as members of the Body of Christ, we must be alert to this tendency and ask God for wisdom, based on the Bible, God's Word for truth and the clarifications and clear understanding of the actual impact of any differences.

8. Core belief in the message of the Gospel must be the basis of all unity.

9. The church group must focus on promoting unity in Christ ... a servant/humble spirit of Service, cooperation and commitment to the Kingdom of God ... "Seek first (primary and highest of our priorities) the Kingdom of God and HIS righteousness ..." and all these things shall be added unto you (among them: UNITY).

10. Accept anyone who gives their life to Christ within one's spiritual family. Paul the Apostle warns us, many times, to watch out for those who want to join but have other intentions, wanting to be important, in charge and the influence to gain their advantage.

CPSIA information can be obtained
at www.ICGtesting.com
Printed in the USA
LVHW02*1531090818
586497LV00006B/35/P

9 781973 634195